Southeastern
Frontiers

BIBLIOGRAPHICAL SERIES
The Newberry Library Center
for the History of the American Indian

General Editor
Francis Jennings

Assistant Editor
William R. Swagerty

The Center Is Supported by Grants from

The National Endowment for the Humanities
The Ford Foundation
The W. Clement and Jessie V. Stone Foundation
The Woods Charitable Fund, Inc.
Mr. Gaylord Donnelley
The Andrew W. Mellon Foundation
The Robert R. McCormick Charitable Trust
The John D. and Catherine T. McArthur Foundation

Southeastern Frontiers: Europeans, Africans, and American Indians, 1513–1840

A Critical Bibliography

JAMES HOWLETT O'DONNELL III

Published for the Newberry Library

Indiana University Press

BLOOMINGTON

Manufactured in the United States of America

Library of Congress Cataloging in Publication Data

O'Donnell, James H., 1937–
    Southeastern frontiers.

    (Bibliographical series / The Newberry Library Center for the History of the American Indian)
    Includes index.
    1. Indians of North America—Southern States—History—Bibliography.   2. Indians of North America—Southern States—First contact with Occidental civilization—Bibliography.   3. Southern States—History—Colonial period, ca. 1600–1775—Bibliography.   4. Southern States—Hisotry—1775–1865—Bibliography.   I. Title.   II. Series: Bibliographical series (Newberry Library. Center for the History of the American Indian).
Z1209.2.U52S666   [E78.S65]   016.975   81–48086
ISBN 0–253–35398–X (pbk.)   AACR2
1 2 3 4 5 86 85 84 83 82

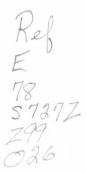

CONTENTS

Editors' Preface vii

Introduction ix

Recommended Works xv

Bibliographical Essay 1

   The First Wave: Spain and the
     Sixteenth-Century Frontier 1

   A Double Wave: Englishmen and Africans 18

   Mounting Tides: Anglo-French
     Expansionism and Conflict 29

   Angry Seas: The American Revolution
     and Early National Period 41

   Removal 50

Alphabetical List and Index 58

EDITOR'S PREFACE

There was a time, not long ago, when a historian of considerable prominence could say that "the South" included only persons of unmixed European ancestry. That is not the definition used in this book or this series. The American Southeast, or "Old South," is today the home of persons whose ancestors came from Africa as well as Europe and met at the shore other persons whose ancestors had lived in the region from time immemorial.

The ways they met and mingled are the subject of this volume. Though Americans are accustomed to think of "the frontier" as a line between peoples of the East and the West, the frontiers of the Southeast were mixed in direction and movement and embraced as well as divided many diverse peoples. They are to be conceived as webs rather than as walls. The Southeast's frontier webs were perhaps more varied than those in any other region of the territories now governed by the United States. Their three great continental stocks were far from homogeneous internally. Spaniards, Frenchmen, Englishmen, and Scots variously struggled and cooperated among themselves and with native Natchez, Timucuans, Creeks, Cherokees, Catawbas, Chickasaws, Seminoles, Yamassees, Tuscaroras, Powhatans, and other tribes who also pursued individual objectives, sometimes in common, sometimes at odds. And the free and slave Africans came from different tribes in their parent continent, about whose transplanted and acquired differences we know very little.

There was also a considerable set of geographical influences in the Southeast that distinguished its frontiers from those of contemporary frontiers in the Northeast. The warm climate that made possible plantations developed with slave labor is obvious. Less obvious, perhaps, were differences in the directions groups faced toward each other. Because English colonies occupied a central position along the Atlantic seaboard, their northern provinces faced toward the French of Canada and the Great Lakes region. The southern English provinces faced toward Spaniards in Florida and Frenchmen in Louisiana. There were thus two great zones of international competition that had little influence upon each other except by way of imperial interests and policies, and the Indian peoples were drawn centripetally into the two vortexes of imperial conflict.

Long before surveyors Mason and Dixon set their famous boundary line, England's northern and southern colonies were self-consciously distinct regions that may be said, in one respect, to have been back-to-back and pulling away from each other. The disastrous consequences of that division are well known, but we need to learn more about the frontiers that played so strong a part in bringing it to pass. Socioeconomic, political, and geographical influences all must be taken into account, and all are addressed in this book.

INTRODUCTION

Almost ninety years ago the historian Frederick J. Turner popularized the use of the "frontier" as a focus for study. Since that time it has been applied to everything from a demographic known—fewer than two persons per square mile in population—to a political metaphor implying challenge, growth, and change. This bibliographical essay links the geographical referent "southeastern" with the term "frontiers" within a time frame of approximately three centuries, 1513–1840.

It is a commonplace that for purposes of organizational, administrative, and academic convenience, the terms, "the South," "southern," and "southeastern United States" usually mean that area within the present United States lying east of the Mississippi River and south of the Ohio River. To be sure, some determine "South" by the length of the growing season, others accept that modern analogue of reality—the road map—which puts this area in the South, and a discriminating few determine the region by whether the local restaurants serve grits with breakfast. More seriously, however, Clark Wissler in defining North American culture areas also specifically describes a "southeastern area." Tradition and convenience, then, weigh heavily in favor of this regional distinction.

The process of following this story is complex. Frontiers, for example, will be used not in any of the single senses indicated above, but as a more inclusive term. As a broad guide, I use Jack Forbes's 1968 definition of the frontier as "an *inter-group contact situation,* that is, any instance of more than momentary contact between two ethnic, cultural, or national groups." It was Forbes's [99] contention that we best understand frontiers if we view them as many-faceted, multicultural interfaces.

On the eve of European intrusion, the lands of the region were inhabited by numerous tribal peoples. Unlike the "widowed land" in the northeast described by Francis Jennings in his *The Invasion of America* [148], the southern frontier beginning at the coastal plain (tidewater if you prefer) and extending westward was the home of perhaps 100,000 persons, perhaps even 1,000,000 or more. As Henry Dobyns has pointed out [85] much needs to be done in reconstructing the population of aboriginal America in any of its regions. On either side of the Mississippi River in 1540, for example, large population clusters described by chroniclers of the Hernado de Soto expedition [29] were found by the Spaniards from 1539 to 1543. Many of these urban centers were gone before the next European visitors arrived. Indeed, the underlying theme of these southern frontiers can be expressed by the metaphor of waves of newcomers undermining and engulfing those already there, much as the tide destroys and renews the sand on a beach.

The figure 100,000 cited above is an extrapolation drawn from statistics available in the third quarter of the eighteenth century. John Reed Swanton, considered by many the dean of southeastern anthropology, estimated there were 170,000 Indians in the aboriginal Southeast [294], while Dobyns has postulated a figure perhaps ten times that [84]. As of about 1775, certain statistics were available as kept by the British Indian Department, which listed warriros per tribe. From those totals a tribal estimate might be reached by multiplying by three, four, or five, depending on which ratio of noncombatants was chosen. In 1775 the major tribes in the South were the Cherokees, with 3,000 warriors, the Chickasaws, with 475 warriors, the Choctaws, with 3,100 warriors, and the Creeks (including the Seminoles), with 3,500 warriors. Given those figures, the demographer can work backward through the decimation of war, disease, and other factors such as alcohol to reach a substantial population estimate for 225 years earlier. To the populations mentioned above would have to be added all the coastal peoples engulfed by the overwhelming tides from across the Atlantic. Timucuans, Apalachees, Guales, Yamassees, Natchez, Houmas, and Chitimachas enumerate only a few of the grains washed away. The Tuscaroras would have met a similar fate, but they emigrated northward into the sanctuary of the Iroquois and managed to survive.

Across these well-established beaches of civilization rolled the first new wave near the middle of the sixteenth century. From north-central Florida north and west across the Gulf plains to the Mississippi River just south of Memphis these Spanish newcomers advanced. When they receded they were not immediately followed by another breaker, but they left behind them destruction in two forms—those they had killed or wounded in fighting, and those who would die from European viruses.

The Spanish *entrada* would not be followed by any attempt at colonization, because no great wealth had been discerned by those who survived to report. Nonetheless, when the tide bore the next major wave upriver in 1607, the English believed they could copy the Spanish success from the land of the Aztecs and go home laden with riches. The wealth was not in precious minerals, however, but in the golden weed the English came to cultivate at the expense of the native population's landholdings. The English, furthermore, brought in the next wave of newcomers—Africans. Blacks had set foot on the southeastern shores with the Spaniards in the previous century, but the English brought them in increasing numbers. By the middle of the eighteenth century there were perhaps 750,000 Blacks living in the southern colonies.

In the meantime the French had become interested in the New World and its peoples and had attempted to settle along the Atlantic shore late in the 1560s. Although rebuffed by the Spaniards in those efforts, in the space of another century they would come to dominate the Mississippi frontier.

Thus, by the early seventeenth century there were present on the southern frontiers in one form or another all the peoples who would from that point on compete for survival. Indigenous peoples such as the

Powhatans, Tuscaroras, Yamassees, Catawbas, Creeks, Timucuans, Guales, Apalachees, Choctaws, Cherokees, Chickasaws, Natchez, Houmas, and Chitimachas were there; the English, French, and Spanish waves were beginning to roll in; and, the Africans were carried unwillingly ashore by the current of European exploitation.

RECOMMENDED WORKS

For the Beginner

[100]   Grant Foreman, *Indian Removal.*

[101]   Grant Foreman, *The Five Civilized Tribes.*

[145]   Charles Hudson, *The Southeastern Indians.*

[212]   Gary B. Nash, *Red, White and Black.*

[329]   J. Leitch Wright, *The Only Land They Knew.*

For a Basic Library

[6]   John R. Alden, *John Stuart and the Southern Colonial Frontier.*

[57]   David Corkran, *The Cherokee Frontier.*

[58]   David Corkran, *The Creek Frontier.*

[66]   Verner W. Crane, *The Southern Frontier.*

[77]   Arthur H. DeRosier, *The Removal of the Choctaw Indians.*

[79]   Louis De Vorsey, *The Indian Boundary in the Southern Colonies.*

[110]   Arrell M. Gibson, *The Chickasaws.*

[216]   James H. O'Donnell, III, *The Southern Indians in the American Revolution.*

[229]   Theda Perdue, *Slavery and the Evolution of Cherokee Society.*

[246]   David B. Quinn, *North America from Earliest Discovery to First Settlements.*

[259]   W. Stitt Robinson, *The Southern Colonial Frontier.*

[269]   Carl Ortwin Sauer, *Sixteenth Century North America.*

[294]   John Reed Swanton, *The Indians of the Southeastern United States.*

[332]   Mary E. Young, *Redskins, Ruffleshirts, and Rednecks.*

BIBLIOGRAPHICAL ESSAY

The First Wave: Spain and the Sixteenth-Century Frontier

Since this essay will focus on the culture-contact history of the southeastern region, beginning with European exploration, readers interested in the earlier history of the area should refer to other bibliographies in this series on the Creeks [119], Cherokees [97], and Choctaws [159]. Two standard reference works are essential for beginning student and advanced scholar alike as overviews of southern Indians' culture. Charles Hudson's *The Southeastern Indians* [145] is an excellent example of successful weaving together of archaeological, ethnographic, and anthropological data. Hudson's ethnohistorical perspective makes this the best overview available of Indians from prehistory to the present, but the book will not satisfy the researcher seeking specific information tribe-by-tribe. For that the work of John R. Swanton, especially his *The Indians of the Southeastern United States* [294], is the best place to turn. Completed in 1946, this 943-page compendium of ethnology, archaeology, history, and ethnography remains the single most important work ever produced on the diverse peoples living within the region. Although Hudson and Swanton disagree over the boundaries that constituted the aboriginal Southeast, the two volumes complement each other and will lead the researcher to a vast body of literature on specific topics. Swanton's encyclopedic *The Indian Tribes of North America* [295] is also a helpful guide.

Spanish explorers may have touched North American shores before 1513 in search of a passage to the East Indies. But, for lack of documentary evidence, the history of contact between tribes of the mainland and expeditionaries fanning out from the Spanish-occupied Caribbean islands is normally associated with Juan Ponce de León's hostile reception among the Calusas of south Florida in 1513. Minor voyages and contacts with the North American coast and its peoples are surveyed in two important syntheses by cultural geographer Carl Ortwin Sauer and historian David Beers Quinn. Sauer's *Sixteenth Century North America* [269] is the product of a lifetime of interest and scholarship by a talented researcher who understood the dynamics of human and nonhuman ecology. Using a chronological framework, Sauer flushed out major themes of Indian-White contact and relations and provides excellent and easily understood analysis of the importance of environmental factors affecting human occupation and interaction on the North American landscape. David Beers Quinn's *North America from Earliest Discovery to First Settlements: The Norse Voyages to 1612* [246] contains more detail on specific meetings of Europeans and Indians in the period before large-scale arrival of non-Southern Europeans to the Western Hemisphere. Quinn's acquaintance with the history of cartography makes this a most informative all-purpose text. Students seeking even greater detail on early Spanish-

Indian contacts will find indispensable Woodbury Lowery's *The Spanish Settlements within the Present Limits of the United States 1513–1574* [177], first published in the early 1900s. Lowery did not benefit from the work of John R. Swanton and his students and therefore is often misleading on identification of the Indian polities he discusses, but this narrative and the accompanying appendixes are sound and have largely stood the test of time as reliable on most aspects of the early Spanish effort to explore and colonize Florida and New Mexico. Another useful introduction is John B. Brebner's *Explorers of North America* [36].

The early history of Spanish efforts to establish beachheads and colonies in the vast region they named La Florida is a story of misfortune, miscalculation, and failure from 1513 to 1565. Juan Ponce de León's two thrusts into the land of the Calusas may be read firsthand in T. Frederick Davis, comp., "History of Juan Ponce de León's Voyages to Florida: Source Records" [69]. Recently David Beers Quinn has edited an extremely useful documentary collection of sixteenth-century voyages of exploration and expeditions under the title *New American World* [248].

Many of the sources for minor expeditions to the Southeast are gleaned from two important Spanish works published in the period when the authors had the advantage of interviewing participants and survivors of Spanish *entradas*. Gonzálo Fernández de Oviedo y Valdés (1478–1557) produced several key historical works on Spanish extension of empire in the

New World. Portions of his magnum opus, *La historia general y natural de las Indias,* were published in Spain during his lifetime. The complete work was not published until the 1850s [222]. Those who can read Spanish will find this four-volume work indispensable. Others can utilize excerpts translated in Quinn's *New American World* [248].

Less important than Oviedo for primary material utilized as oral history, but equally significant as an overview of Spanish interest in the North American frontier to their north, is the work of Antonio de Herrera y Tordesillas (1559– 1625). His *Historia general de los hechos de los castellaños en las islas i tierra firme del mar oceano* [131] appeared in four volumes between 1601 and 1615. The researcher with language skills is urged to consult this detailed history, if only to gain an understanding of how Spanish officials and colonials viewed their northern frontiers vis-à-vis other parts of the Spanish empire in the Americas. Herrera was the official historian of the crown and therefore lacked objectivity on many matters including Spanish-Indian relations; but, his work, like that of Oviedo, is a statement of Spain's relentless dedication to recording the history of deeds and notable events in the lives of her sons and daughters throughout the world. Much of what is known about New World colonial society and the cultures of the various Indian peoples of the southern half of the United States is the result of this devotion.

Students of southeastern frontiers will find two expeditions of special interest for understanding Indian-White relations in the sixteenth century. The

first was officially described as that led by Pánfilo de
Narváez in 1528, but it is best known for the account
written by one of the handful of survivors who managed to return to Spanish civilization some six years later. Originally published in 1542, the *Relation* of Álvar
Núñez Cabeza de Vaca has been made widely available
in various editions. This important primary source for
the ethnogeography of Indian tribes of Florida, the
lower Mississippi Valley, Texas, and northern Mexico is
of special value in that many of the cultures visited by
the Vaca party were not revisited until one hundred or,
in some cases, two hundred years later. And, when
they were, vast changes had occurred. Much of our
knowledge of the Karankawas and Coahuitecans of
present-day Texas derives from Núñez's reconstruction
of his life as slave, trader-emissary, shaman-healer, and
distinguished visitor during his peregrinations. The
most useful of his account is that translated by Fanny
Bandelier with notes by her husband, the famous Swiss
anthropologist Adolph F. Bandelier [214]. The Spanish
text is most readily available in the two-volume edition
prepared by Manuel Serrano y Sanz [272]. Frederick
Webb Hodge edited the *Relation* for inclusion in the
Original Narratives of Early American History series in
1907 [133]. Recently the Bandeliers' version has been
reissued with Oviedo's version of the official report on
the expedition, the latter translated by Gerald Theisen
with an introduction by John Francis Bannon [298].

The second expedition of special note, and that
which had the greatest impact upon Indian peoples
throughout the region, was led by Hernando de Soto

and his successor, Luis de Moscoso, between 1539 and 1543. A great deal of time, energy, and ink has been devoted to retracing Soto's route and to unraveling the mysteries that continue to perplex scholars concerned with the tribal/cultural affiliations of many of the more than one hundred polities that occupied the lands through which the Spaniards marched. Three accounts by participants have survived, as well as one important letter written by Soto and a reconstruction based upon interviews with survivors by Garcilaso de la Vega, an early chronicler of mixed Indian and Spanish heritage. The most important of these is the *True Relation . . . by a Gentleman of Elvas.* First published in Portuguese in 1577, the best translated edition is that of James A. Robertson [257]. The first English attempt at translation by Richard Hakluyt in 1609, published as *Virginia Richly Valued* [121] is adequate. The 1861 effort at translation by Buckingham Smith was reprinted in Edward Gaylor Bourne, ed., *Narratives of the Career of Hernando de Soto* [29], and in Hodge and Lewis, eds., *Spanish Explorers in the Southern United States, 1528– 1543* [173]. Smith's translation is unreliable and should not be used by the serious scholar; however, Bourne's second volume of the Trailmaker Series publication contains the eyewitness accounts of Rodrigo Ranjel, Soto's private secretary, translated from Oviedo, and Smith's translation of Luys Hernández de Biedma's version. Other source material may be found in the "Hernando de Soto Number" of the *Florida Historical Quarterly* [330] and in Benjamin F. French, ed. *Histori-*

cal Collections of Louisiana [105]. The latter contains an important letter written by Soto, French's version of Biedma's relation, and a reprint of Hakluyt's 1609 Elvas narrative.

The Florida of the Inca [303], translated and edited by John Grier Varner and Jeanette Johnson Varner, is the best version of this early seventeenth-century publication, which purports to contain eyewitness accounts written down "to the letter" by Garcilaso. The veracity of the history is open to question, but much of it is corroborated by other primary accounts and by ethnological information gathered and analyzed at later dates. John R. Swanton in "The Ethnological Value of the De Soto Narratives" [292] enumerates the contributions of Garcilaso's history for understanding southeastern cultures. Other evaluators, especially José B. Hernández in "Opposing Views of La Florida: Álvar Núñez Cabeza de Vaca and El Inca Garcilaso de la Vega" [130], are less forgiving of the literary license taken by this descendant of Incan nobility. Hernández draws useful comparisons between Núñez's reaction to La Florida, hardly a paradise in his estimation, and the romanticized Arcadia described at times by Garcilaso. The careful researcher will want to read Garcilaso with two important reference works close at hand. Foremost is the *Final Report of the United States De Soto Expedition Commission,* chaired by John R. Swanton in the 1930s [293]. This contains useful tables, maps, linguistic analyses, and an in-depth discussion of the route. Interpretations by various students of Soto's trek are also included up to 1939, though much debate continues on this intriguing subject. As a second reference work, any researcher who plunges into the Soto expedition narratives will want to have Swanton's *Indians of the Southeastern United States* [294] nearby. Scholars will also find of value Swanton's *Early History of the Creek Indians and Their Neighbors* [290], his *Indian Tribes of the Lower Mississippi Valley and Adjacent Coast of the Gulf of Mexico* [289], and his *Source Material for the Social and Ceremonial Life of the Choctaw Indians* [291].

Archaeological investigations retracing Soto's route have produced limited results. Many of the large temple-mound villages visited by the Spaniards have not been correlated with the documentary sources, and there is much disagreement over the route on most segments of the trek across the southern portion of the United States. In addition to the *Final Report*, those seeking technical reports will want to inspect Phillips, Ford, and Griffin, "Archaeological Survey in the Lower Mississippi Alluvial Valley, 1940–1947" [230], and Brain, Toth, and Rodriguez-Buckingham, "Ethnohistoric Archaeology and the Desoto Entrada into the Lower Mississippi Valley" [35]. Although the primary direction of the latter is archaeo-anthropological, the authors draw upon a number of methods to review the literature and to reconstruct the most plausible route for the expedition in the still-perplexing area of Mississippi and Alabama. In the course of these discussions, much information about the interaction between Spaniards and native peoples is suggested that is useful to the historian. The verdict is not in on Soto's route nor the often disastrous effect produced by man and disease upon Indians throughout the region. Projects at major universities in Georgia, Alabama, and South Carolina continue to produce stimulating new hypotheses on Soto's route and the size and specifics of villages visited.

The Spanish expeditions that followed Soto's explorations in the second half of the sixteenth century are analyzed and made available for documentary use in Quinn, *North America from Earliest Discovery to First Settlements* [246], and Quinn, ed., *New American World* [248]. Those researchers interested in expeditions to the region of Guale on the Georgia and South Carolina coasts will find Paul Quattlebaum's *The Land Called Chicora* [244] a useful analysis covering the period from the 1520s to 1670. On Tristán de Luna's ill-fated attempts to settle Florida in the 1560s, Herbert I. Priestley has edited a near-definitive collection under the title *The Luna Papers, 1559–1561* [241]. The bilingual researcher will delight in finding the Spanish version printed alongside the translation. Priestley's biography of Luna [240] is also of use, especially for understanding the motivations of Spanish colonists who eagerly migrated to North America, only to find life not all that easy on Florida's shores.

The story of French incursions into lands claimed by Spain has been the subject of a number of historians, many of whom have distorted the story of international rivalry and the "massacre" of the Huguenot garrison at Fort Caroline on the eastern side of the Florida peninsula in 1565. Documentary sources for that struggle are found in Jean Ribaut's *Whole and True Discouerye* (1563) [255] and in René Goulaine de Laudonnière, *L'histoire notable de la Floride* (1586), the latter being available in translation as *Three Voyages*, prepared by Charles E. Bennett [168]. *Laudonnière and Fort Caroline: History and Documents*, edited by Charles E. Bennett [22], contains a brief but useful history and several accounts of the French colony from 1562 to 1565. Stefan Lorant has printed the accounts of Jacques le Moyne de Morgues, whose version was illustrated by Theodore de Bry originally in 1591. The Le Moyne narrative and that of the colony's surviving carpenter, Nicolas Le Challeaux, are translated in Lorant's *The New World: Notes on the French Settlements in Florida, 1562–1565* [176].

Much information on various Indian groups visited by the French is found in the European narratives, especially those of Laudonnière and Le Moyne. Analysis of relations between European invaders and Timucuans, the linguistic stock of peoples occupying the area of contention in northern Florida, is the focus of James W. Covington's "Relations between the Eastern Timucuan Indians and the French and Spanish, 1564– 1567" [64]. Two important summaries of archaeological and historical information on Timucuans are found in Jerald T. Milanich and Samuel Proctor, eds., *Tacachale: Essays on the Indians of Florida and Southern Georgia during the Historic Period* [200]. "Cultures in

Transition: Fusion and Assimilation among the Eastern Timucua" [71], by Kathleen A. Deagan, and "The Western Timucua: Patterns of Acculturation and Change" [199], by Jerald T. Milanich, discuss the Timucuans from archaeological and ethnohistorical perspectives. Deagan's contribution is especially instructive for understanding the decline of Indian population under the Spanish mission system of the seventeenth and eighteenth centuries.

The founding of Saint Augustine and the occupation of Florida and the Gulf Coast by Spaniards from 1565 on have been the focus of numerous scholars. No sooner had Pedro Menéndez de Avilés rid Charles V of Lutherans in his lands than historians began writing histories of the notable event in Spanish history. Two important works completed in the 1560s are worth inspecting. Bartolomé Barrientos's *Vida y hechos de Pero Menéndez de Avilés* was made accessible by Genaro García in his work *Dos Antiguas Relaciónes de la Florida* [107]. A recent translation by Anthony Kerrigan [16] is recommended. Gonzalo Solís de Merás, a member of the punitive expeditionary force under Menéndez wrote a second biography of the conquest of Florida in the 1560s. His account is available in Spanish in Eugenio Ruidíaz y Caravia, *La Florida: Su conquista y colonización por Pedro Menéndez de Avilés* [267], and in an English edition translated by Jeannette Connor [279]. Menéndez's personal correspondence is a large manuscript collection, much of which has not been published. Ruidíaz y Caravia published a sizable portion of his letters to officials in *La Florida* and used them for his own personal interpretation of the conquest in volume 1 of the set. Henry Ware translated seven letters from Menéndez to the Spanish crown in a volume of the *Proceedings of the Massachusetts Historical Society* in 1894 [194]. It is to be regretted that Edward Lawson's translations of most of the extant Menéndez correspondence remain in typescript in the University of Florida Library.

An early eighteenth-century Spanish historian pieced together the story of Florida's Spanish beginnings in a remarkably detailed and, for the most part, accurate history of events to 1722. Andrés González de Barcia Carballido y Zuñiga's *Ensayo cronológica para la historia general de la Florida* (1723) was translated through the able hand of Anthony Kerrigan [14]. Barcia relied heavily upon Barrientos and Solís de Merás but fills in many gaps where the documentary record is scant. Francis Parkman's nineteenth-century publication *Pioneers of France in the New World* [223] promoted Hispanophobic and highly subjective stereotypes of rapacious and greedy Spaniards under Menéndez de Avilés killing innocent Huguenots in Florida, and it should be read only as historical fiction by those interested in mastery of literary style and techniques of distorting documents. A much sounder discussion by a modern historian is Eugene Lyon, *The Enterprise of Florida* [179]. Lyon has combed the Spanish archives and makes a very complex story less ambiguous and more understandable in the context of the sixteenth century. His discussions of Spanish institutions and the procedural manner by which exploration and colonization advanced into North America are lucid and instructive for those confused by the mode and means of New World Spanish ventures. Researchers interested specifically in Indian-White relations will find James W. Covington's "Relations between the Eastern Timucuan Indians and the French and Spanish, 1564–1567" [64], John J. TePaske's "Spanish Indian Policy and the Struggle for Empire in the Southeast, 1513–1776" [297], and William C. Sturtevant "Spanish-Indian Relations in Southeastern North America" [286] useful.

Menéndez de Avilés succeeded where his predecessors had failed in maintaining settlements on North American soil. The precursors of two essential institutions in the Spanish formula of frontier colonization were his primary goals. One worked; the other faltered and eventually failed entirely until new strategies were used. The one that worked was the fortress-block-house-presidio analyzed by Verne E. Chatelain in *The Defenses of Spanish Florida, 1565–1763* [51]; the one that failed was missionary enterprise under the Society of Jesus. During Menéndez's rule of Florida (1565–74), Jesuits attempted to live within Indian villages or on their periphery with a minimum of protection by Spanish soldiers. Owing to alienation of Indian populations by military and civilian personnel, martyrdom became commonplace for the followers of Loyola who were assigned to Florida. Félix Zubillaga has written an excellent history of this effort in *La Florida: La misión*

Jesuítica (1566–1572) y la colonización española [336].
Those able to read Latin will find Zubillaga's edited
work *Monumenta Antiquae Floridae (1566–1572)* [337]
indispensable for understanding the history of
Indian-White relations. The northernmost Jesuit effort
around modern-day Chesapeake Bay is the subject of
Clifford M. Lewis and Albert J. Loomie, *The Spanish
Jesuit Mission in Virginia, 1570–1572* [172]. All the
known documents for this ill-starred venture that led
to the martyrdom of the priests assigned to minister
among tribes of present-day Virginia are found in this
handsomely printed and excellently translated work.
Secular letters and inquiries, with testimony of soldiers,
colonists, and officials on the infant and near-starving
Florida settlements from 1570 to 1580, have been
translated by Jeanette Connor and published in two
volumes as *Colonial Records of Spanish Florida* [53].

Despite the failures of the Jesuits, the mendicants
did not give up their effort to convert the Indians of
La Florida. Maynard Geiger presents a good narrative
history of new strategies in *The Franciscan Conquest of
Florida (1573–1618)* [109]. Geiger was a Franciscan himself, and his history is less than objective, especially in
discussion of Indian cultures; nonetheless, it is an important chronological history of the mission frontier
and gives the reader a good sense of the traumatic
changes brought about by the creation of mission
complexes designed to congregate previously independent Indian polities for the purpose of Christianization
and acculturation to European lifeways. Anyone seri-

ously interested in the Spanish mission as an institution of the frontier should read Herbert Eugene Bolton's classic statement published in the *American Historical Review* in 1917 [25]. The mission was seen as a pioneering agency that ensured Spain's tenuous and defensive, but nonetheless effective, expansion and resilience to outside pressures during most of the colonial era. Robert A. Matter's "Missions in the Defense of Spanish Florida, 1566–1710" [191] expands upon Bolton's thesis, arguing, as the title implies, that missions served a dual purpose in ensuring Spain's occupancy of North American lands. Those readers interested in origins and backgrounds of the Southeast's First European colonists should see Neasham, "Spain's Emigrants to the New World" [213].

One of the better texts published on New Spain's northern frontiers is John Francis Bannon, *The Spanish Borderlands Frontier, 1513–1821* [11]. A student of Bolton and a Franciscan, Father Bannon provides the reader with excellent conceptual and chronological discussions of themes of "Borderlands" history. The mission frontier is nicely surveyed, though often the reader yearns to learn more about Indian civilization and the interchange of Indian and White culture in the cloistered mission environment.

Spanish expansion beyond present-day Florida into frontier zones of the Muskhogean-speaking Southeast is the subject of John Tate Lanning's *The Spanish Missions of Georgia* [164]. This well-documented history will lead the researcher to key sources, but it does not, unfortunately, tell much about the various Indian neophytes who made continued mission work possible. For that the researcher can turn to Hale G. Smith's *The European and the Indian* [276] and "Spanish-Indian Relationships" [277], as well as *Francisco Pareja's 1613 Confessionario: A Documentary Source for Timucuan Ethnography* [201]. Smith's works correlate archaeological investigations with the historical record, and Pareja's manual gives a good impression of methods used for changing value systems among mission Indians.

Not all Indians of Spanish Florida accepted the mission system without coercion. Seeds of discontent were present from the arrival of the Franciscans in the 1570s. Rebellion festered and eventually erupted in several major revolts, the most important being that associated with the Guale country in the 1590s. Luís Gerónimo de Oré, *The Martyrs of Florida, 1513–1616* [221], completed in the early seventeenth century, contains a chapter on the Guale revolt written by a Franciscan contemporary of those priests who served their order in Florida. A good history of the revolt and Indian responses to European incursions remains to be written. Lewis H. Larson, "Historic Guale Indians of the Georgia Coast and the Impact of the Spanish Mission Effort" [166], is a recent contribution in ethnoarchaeology. It is a good introduction to the resistance discussed by J. G. Johnson in "The Yamassee Revolt of 1597 and the Destruction of the Georgia Missions" [150].

Mary Ross in "The Restoration of the Spanish Missions in Georgia, 1598–1606" [263] provides the sequel to the temporarily successful Guale revolt. Mark F. Boyd's "Mission Sites in Florida" [31], "Further Consideration of the Apalachee Missions" [32], and *Here They Once Stood: The Tragic End of the Apalachee Missions* [33] cover the other side of Florida's mission frontier. Boyd also contributed to our understanding of the expansion of the Hispano-Indian mission empire in his "Expedition of Marcus Delgado from Apalache to the Upper Creek Country in 1686" [30], an article complemented by Fred L. Pearson, Jr., "The Arguelles Inspection of Guale" [225]. Both Boyd and Pearson provide accounts of the Spanish expeditions of the seventeenth century in lands ignored for over a hundred years. Some commentary on native peoples is provided, and Pearson is helpful in cataloging the number of villages visited and the languages spoken. James W. Covington's "Apalachee Indians, 1704–1763" [63] describes the bumping of peoples along the frontier after English colonists began raiding Spanish territory for Indian slaves. He recounts the destruction of the Apalachee towns and the removal of many of the inhabitants to Georgia, as well as the impact on the peoples of the entire region during the major resistance effort known as the Yamassee War (1715–17), which ended in flight westward by Apalachees toward Pensacola and Mobile. Warfare in this period is examined by Barbara A. Purdy in "Weapons, Strategies, and Tactics of the Europeans and the Indians in 16th and 17th Century Florida" [243]. Likewise instructive on the European context of activities in the Southeast is John Tate Lanning's *The Diplomatic History of Georgia* [165].

The Florida Gulf Coast frontier is the subject of Irving A. Leonard's *Spanish Approaches to Pensacola, 1689–1693* [170], which contains twenty useful documents, and William Edward Dunn's *Spanish and French Rivalry in the Gulf Region of the United States, 1678–1702* [89]. Lawrence Kinnaird, *Spain in the Mississippi Valley, 1765–1794* [161]; Duvon Corbitt, "Papers from the Spanish Archives Relating to Tennessee and the Old Southwest, 1783– 1800" [56]; and Corbitt's "Papers Relating to the Georgia-Florida Frontier, 1784– 1800" [55] contain the fundamental sorce records for Spanish extension westward and toward the north during the eighteenth century. Henry Folmer, *Franco-Spanish Rivalry in North America, 1524–1763* [98], is a good interpretive overview of the contest for empire in the Southeast.

A Double Wave: Englishmen and Africans

Some four decades after the native peoples in the South encountered the European intruders from Spain, they began to be visited by nationals of both France and Great Britain. British interest lay somewhat northward, away from the Spaniards in the area of Cape Hatteras and Chesapeake Bay. Accounts of British visitation and arrival toward the close of the sixteenth century may be found in two major works by David B. Quinn: the first is an edited collection of documents entitled *The Roanoke Voyages, 1584–1590* [247]; the second is an interpretive work, *England and the Dis-*

covery of America, 1481–1620: From the Bristol Voyages of the Fifteenth Century to the Pilgrim Settlement in Plymouth [245]. One of the early visitors at Roanoke left a memorable artistic record that is succinctly described in David I. Bushnell, "John White—the First English Artist to Visit America, 1585" [41]. Some of White's excellent drawings are available in Stefan Lorant, ed., *The New World* [176], but the most complete and recent publication treating White as artist, natural historian, and cartographer is Paul Hulton and David B. Quinn, *The American Drawings of John White, 1577–1590* [146].

At about the same time as the native peoples greeted the English newcomers to their lands, they were also welcoming arrivals from France. Late sixteenth-century activity by the French was focused principally along the south Atlantic coast in present-day South Carolina and Georgia, the region held by Spain as part of La Florida. A study of French activities that needs revision in light of modern data and research techniques is Mary Ross, "French Intrusions and Indian Uprisings in Georgia and South Carolina, 1577–1580" [261]. Fanciful illustrations of the French interactions with the native peoples were recorded by the French artist Jacques LeMoyne. Engravings of his work by the Flemish artisan Theodore De Bry became widely known in Europe, but neither the painter nor his imitator possessed an eye for recording equal to that of John White. The sole surviving LeMoyne painting and over forty De Bry engravings may be found in the revised edition of Lorant [176]. Those seeking visual material with superb ethnographic detail will find the work of A. DeBatz important. Some of his art has been analyzed and reproduced by David I. Bushnell [40]. DeBatz's sketches of the Indians along the lower Mississippi are particularly instructive for identifying different tribal peoples as well as an African who was living among the natives.

By 1610 the native peoples of the southern frontiers found themselves confronted by sizable groups of newcomers with strange views about the New World. For a discussion of certain aspects of the intellectual baggage brought by the Europeans, see Howard Mumford Jones, *O Strange New World* [152]. The same subject has been explored at length from another perspective in the collected papers of a Renaissance studies conference edited by Fredi Chiappelli as *First Images of America: The Impact of the New World on the Old* [52]. Other "first images" are found in Hugh Honour, *The New Golden Land* [140]. Static and dynamic concepts of European nations about the background of native peoples may be explored in Lee E. Huddleston, *Origins of the American Indians: European Concepts, 1492–1729* [144]. How these ideas were transferred into the English colonial perception has been traced by Gary B. Nash in "The Image of the Indian in the Southern Colonial Mind" [211]. Nash wrote that "in America the image of the Indian was molded by the nature of colonization and the inner requirements of adventuring Englishmen." Similarly, Roy Harvey Pearce in *The Savages of America: A Study of the Indian and the Idea of Civili-*

zation [224] argued that the Indian's importance to the English mind lay not in himself but in showing civilized men what they must not be.

The most recent discussion of European perceptions of native peoples in early Virginia is Bernard Sheehan, *Savagism and Civility: Indians and Englishmen in Colonial Virginia* [274]. Sheehan has combed seventeenth-century English intellectual history to formulate an interpretation of how Elizabethans perceived native Americans as savages even before the first colony was planted in Virginia, and how this perceptual vision persisted in spite of the realities of day-to-day contact between the two civilizations. As intellectual history the book is a strong contribution to understanding the literature of the period, but as a balanced account of Indian-White relations it falls far short. Sheehan has not altered his fundamental position, assumed in *Seeds of Extinction* [273], that he writes from the White man's point of view because "the initiative in Indian-White relations remained predominately with the white man."

In "'Expulsion of the Salvages': English Policy and the Virginia Massacre of 1622" [304], Alden T. Vaughan also accepts the savagism/civility dichotomy as fundamental in his general explanation of Indian-White relations during the initial years of the first permanent English intrusion among native Americans. An older article dealing with the same subject is Wesley F. Craven, "Indian Policy in Early Virginia" [67]. Since neither Craven, Sheehan, nor Vaughan reflects the rigorous application of modern ethnohistorical method, there is certainly room for more work concerning the peoples of early Virginia.

Nancy O. Lurie, however, has given us an extremely helpful analysis of native perceptions of European newcomers in her "Indian Cultural Adjustment to European Civilization" [178], one of several important articles in *Seventeenth-Century America: Essays in Colonial History*, edited by James Morton Smith. The same volume also contains "The Moral and Legal Justifications for Dispossessing the Indians" [310] by Wilcomb E. Washburn. In a sense these two essays portray the yin and yang of early cultural interaction on the Anglo-Indian frontiers.

Further understanding of the problems along these early frontiers may be gained from a number of sources. The once widely maligned Captain John Smith has had much of his credibility restored through the efforts of Philip L. Barbour in *The Three Worlds of Captain John Smith* [12]. For those who want to know Smith's social background, there are details about the captain's home village in Ian Beckwith, "Captain John Smith: the Yeoman Background" [20]. The Pocahontas episode is one of many facets explored by Barbour in attempting to reconstruct the life of the ill-fated young heroine of *Pocahontas and Her World* [13]. Additional insight into early English settlement patterns in America may be gained from Carville V. Earle, "The First English Towns of North America" [90].

The socioeconomic and political context in which Smith and his successors functioned has been carefully described by Edmund Morgan in two articles on early Jamestown that were published in 1971: "The Labor Problem at Jamestown" [206] and "The First American Boom: Virginia, 1618–1630" [205]. The labor problem at Jamestown that Smith had noted so carefully in his writings is elaborated by Morgan along with the additional explanation that much work in early Virginia was left undone in part because of a fundamental English attitude about work and an unfulfilled expectation, based on the Spanish experience, that a labor force would be available from among the indigenous peoples. It appears, then, that English intellectual baggage shaped not only attitudes toward the native Americans but attitudes toward the land itself and what was to be expected of life in the New World. The same theme of labor supply and exploitation was followed by Morgan in his essay "The First American Boom" [205] and more recently in his book *American Slavery, American Freedom* [207]. While these studies do not deal with the Indian-White frontier in any direct way, the demand for labor and land that fueled the boom had clear long-term implications for native American groups living on the frontiers of Virginia's expansion, a point well analyzed by Morgan.

A useful companion to Morgan is Bernard Bailyn's "Politics and Social Structure in Colonial Virginia" [9]. The same problem is approached from a different perspective by Nicholas Canny in "The Permissive Frontier: The Problem of Social Control in English Settlements in Ireland and Virginia, 1550–1660" [43]. In this refreshing comparative essay, Canny argues that "the colonies that emerged were far from the models in civil living that had been intended, since the organizers had been forced by circumstances to accept patterns of settlement radically different from those originally envisioned." In Virginia, many early settlers deserted the colony to live with local Indians, who were used to granting outsiders asylum and residential privileges. The average settlers planted themselves haphazardly in dispersed farm hamlets, disregarding civil regulations and the proprietary plans. As J. Frederick Fausz demonstrated recently in his dissertation "The Powhatan Uprising of 1622" [93] and in an article on the same subject [94], this second factor contributed significantly to tensions over prime croplands and accounts in part for the Powhatan uprising and execution of many European settlers in 1622. Before the uprising and in the reemergence of English strength after the revolt, the expanding settlements introduced the local Indian populations to European legal practices (for better or for worse), a theme explored by Yasuhide Kawashima, "The Native American and White Man's Law before 1800" [155].

During the early years of the seventeenth century, yet another group of newcomers arrived to contribute to the multicultural southern frontiers. These were the Africans, brought in by their Spanish, Dutch, French, and English masters. After the establishment of European outposts in southeastern North America, enslaved Africans were brought into the frontier context. How the Africans interacted as cultural forces vis-à-vis others on the frontiers may be traced in several articles published in the *Journal of Negro History*. Especially important articles are Jerome W. Jones, "The Established Virginia Church and the Conversion of Negroes and Indians, 1620–1760" [154], and James H. Johnston, "Documentary Evidence of Relations of Negroes and Indians" [151]. The primary emphasis of the Jones article is on plans, statutes, and official discussions concerning the "possible" conversion of the Indians and Blacks. The period covered is primarily the early eighteenth century, but there are references to the seventeenth century. The Johnston study is an older account that surveys the field in a superficial way, ranging from the seventeenth century to the nineteenth century. Free Blacks in the colonial Southeast are the focus of Ross M. Kimmel's case study of seventeenth century Maryland [160].

A scholar who has spent much of his career researching Black Americans on the frontiers is Kenneth W. Porter. His articles pertaining to southern frontiers that first appeared in the *Journal of Negro History* are now reprinted, with others, in *The Negro on the American Frontier* [238]. Of particular interest to the student of southeastern frontiers are "Relations between Negroes and Indians within the Present Limits of the United States" [232]; "Notes Supplementary to 'Relations between Negroes and Indians'" [233]; and "Negroes on the Southern Frontier, 1670–1763" [236]. Porter's works are the first useful surveys of the subject, and, while not exhaustive or analytical, they are of major use as introductions to the literature. A more recent foray into the African-Indian frontier is Daniel Littlefield, *Africans and Creeks: From the Colonial Period to the Civil War* [174]. Littlefield deals with contact between the Creeks and Africans over a lengthy period in greater detail than Porter's articles, but his basic chrononarrative approach is the same. There is little ethnohistorical analysis of either Africans or Creeks, a failing that leaves room for further research and analysis into this facet of multiethnic frontiers.

An older essay of related interest is Edgar L. Pennington, "The Reverend Francis Le Jau's Work among Indians and Negro Slaves" [227]. Pennington described not only matters relating to the conversion of the two groups, but also White mistreatment of native peoples, particularly that by traders who took Indian slaves or instigated Indian wars to obtain more slaves.

Specific studies of Blacks as participants in the dynamic interaction of the frontiers have appeared frequently in recent years: Richard Halliburton, Jr., *Red over Black: Black Slavery among the Cherokee Indians* [123], and a popularized article by a similar title [124]; Jack D. L. Holmes, "The Role of Blacks in Spanish Alabama: The Mobile District, 1780–1813" [137]; Theda Perdue, *Slavery and the Evolution of Cherokee Society, 1540–1855* [229]; and J. Leitch Wright, Jr., "Blacks in British East Florida" [327].

While the Holmes essay approaches the subject primarily from the involvement in day-to-day affairs during the period, the Wright study goes slightly beyond in suggesting that, in addition to the Blacks living within the colonial White society, there were also Blacks living among the Indians. Unfortunately, neither in this essay nor in his *Florida in the American Revolution* [326] does Wright provide much information on this subject. In the book he is content to assert that "Blacks also lived among the Indians, either as slaves or freemen."

The most successful of the studies mentioned above is Perdue's *Slavery and the Evolution of Cherokee Society* [229]. From her thorough understanding of the literature she draws upon materials to illustrate her explanation of the presence of slavery in Cherokee society. She moves swiftly from the European invasion to the middle of the nineteenth century, recounting Cherokee responses to outside pressure or internal tensions stemming from slavery.

When the first African runaway stumbled breathlessly into an Indian village somewhere in the South, his story was probably no shock to the villagers. Slavery was practiced by the native American peoples long before the Eurpeans arrived. Before 1780, however, it was a different kind of enslavement, since slavery in native American societies did not carry the same onus as it did in the Old World. A former slave might achieve a new life as a member of the tribe to which he or she fled. Given the widespread practice of adoption among these tribal peoples, it was not difficult for an African to find a place in tribal life and leadership. The problem of runaways and the response of colonial governments is the subject of John TePaske, "The Fugitive Slave: Intercolonial Rivalry and Spanish Slave Policy, 1697–1764" [296].

Because of this skill at adaptation by native peoples, one is somewhat troubled by William S. Willis's "Divide and Rule: Red, White, and Black in the Southeast" [319]. In part Willis proceeds from the assumption that only the Whites could manipulate. There is evidence that native peoples were as capable of this as Europeans when it came to capturing runaways and then threatening to keep them or sell them at auction if the reward offered was too low. A sophisticated work about the slave side of the issue from the point of view of the Africans and their aims is the brilliant work *Black Majority: Negroes in Colonial South Carolina from 1670 through the Stono Rebellion* [320] by Peter Wood.

It is perhaps because the native peoples had their own particular form of slavery and also understood what happened to Black slaves kept by Europeans that attempts to enslave Indians met with extremely limited success. In general the literature on the subject is dated or of little use. The most recent work is Donald Grinde's "Native American Slavery in the Southern Colonies" [120]. Grinde's article is weighted in a particular way and must be used with care. Also of recent vintage is Russell M. Magnaghi, "The Role of Indian Slavery in Colonial St. Louis" [187]. Magnaghi's article is of particular interest because it deals with multiethnic frontiers. The only general work on this subject is dated and much in need of replacement with one following modern research methods: Almon W. Lauber, *Indian Slavery in Colonial Times within the Present Limits of the United States* [167].

Mounting Tides: Anglo-French Expansion and Conflict

With the increase of peoples on the frontiers of the South, it might be expected that conflict would arise. Indeed, by the third quarter of the seventeenth century Virginia's expansion was increasing the dynamic interaction of peoples along a number of interfaces. Hugh Jones's *The Present State of Virginia* [153] is a good contemporary history of the colony at the end of its first century. For a basic discussion of English motives and aims in this period the researcher should consult three works by Wilcomb E. Washburn: *The Governor and the Rebel: A History of Bacon's Rebellion in Virginia* [308]; "The Effect of Bacon's Rebellion on Government in England and Virginia" [311]; and "Governor Berkeley and King Philip's War" [309]. Also of significance in this connection are W. Neil Franklin's "Virginia and the Cherokee Indian Trade, 1673–1752" [103] and its sequel, "Virginia and the Cherokee Indian Trade, 1753–1775" [104]. Franklin's emphasis is on the trader and the economics of trade, which says little about the impact of trade on Cherokee material culture. Attention should also be given to W. Stitt Robinson's "Indian Education and Missions in Colonial

Virginia" [258]. Robinson traces the plans and funding for Indian education but does not assess its effect. He records the money available and reports the presence of a few young Indians at the College of William and Mary.

As Virginia reached westward, so too did South Carolina. The Carolina story is still best told in Verner W. Crane, *The Southern Frontier, 1670–1732* [66]. Although the study is White-centered with an emphasis on European expansion, politics, and economics, it is so thorough that it remains a useful handbook of the period. A more recent analysis of the frontier by a scholar attuned to native American presence in the region is W. Stitt Robinson, *The Southern Colonial Frontier* [259].

The Spanish response to the outreach of the English colonials may be followed by reading two general studies and some shorter articles: Herbert E. Bolton and Mary Ross, *The Debatable Land* [27]; J. Leitch Wright, Jr., *Anglo-Spanish Rivalry in North America* [325]; Wright's "Spanish Reaction to Carolina" [323]; and Herbert E. Bolton, "Spanish Resistance to Carolina Traders in Western Georgia, 1608–1704" [26]. Although there is a difference in time of publication for these studies, they are similar in that the authors share a view of the frontier as a stage for international diplomacy. They should be given consideration since the imperial aims of the European powers were often translated into economic competition and warfare destructive of native societies in the long run.

One interesting and largely unexplored aspect of comparative frontiers in North America is Spain's ability to interact with native peoples without resorting to the treaties negotiated by the English and the French. This was the subject of Charles Gibson's presidential address to the American Historical Association in 1977: "Conquest, Capitulation, and Indian Treaties" [111]. With Howard Peckham, Gibson edited another work appropriate for consideration in this context: *Attitudes of Colonial Powers toward the American Indian* [226].

By the time the native peoples interacted with the English, Spanish, and African peoples in the South, they were at the point of being joined by the French. Early attempts at colonization by France along the southern Atlantic coast had met little success, but by late in the seventeenth century parties of Frenchmen had descended the Mississippi and begun to march across the Gulf plains. From 1682 to 1683, La Salle and his party made their historic descent of the Mississippi, encountering numbers of native societies. The best brief original account is that by Henri Tonty, "Memoir Sent in 1693, on the Discovery of the Mississippi and the Neighboring Nations by M. De La Salle, from the Year 1678 to the Time of His Death, and by the Sieur de Tonty to the Year 1691," in Louise Phelps Kellogg, *Early Narratives of the Northwest, 1634–1699* [158]. Tonty's mission to the Chickasaws has been examined by Jay Higginbotham in "Henri de Tonti's Mission to the Chickasaw, 1702" [132].

Other primary sources recording contemporary impressions of the several peoples on the frontiers of French-African-Indian contact in the lower Mississippi are Bernard de La Harpe, *Journal historique de l'establissement des français à la Louisiane* [163]; Jean Champigny, *The Present State of . . . Louisiana* [50]; Antoine LePage du Pratz, *The History of Louisiana* [171]; and Dunbar Rowland and A. G. Sanders, *Mississippi Provincial Archives: The French Dominion* [265]. Several drawings portraying natives and their cultures along the Mississippi were completed by A. DeBatz in the 1730s. As noted earlier, these are available in David I. Bushnell, *Drawings by A. DeBatz in Louisiana, 1732–1735* [40]. A journal kept by a French visitor to the Cherokee country in the early 1740s is the "Journal of Antoine Bonnefoy" [28].

Secondary treatments of a general nature about French-Indian frontiers may be found in Louise P. Kellogg, "France and the Mississippi Valley" [157]; John R. McDermott, *The French in the Mississippi Valley* [181]; W. J. Eccles, *France in America* [91]; Mary Ross, "The French on the Savannah, 1605" [262]; and Mason Wade, "The French and the Indians" [306]. Two specific Franco-Indian problems are dealt with in short essays by Norman W. Caldwell, "Chickasaw Threat to French Control of the Mississippi in the 1740's" [42], and R. G. McWilliams, "Iberville and the Southern Indians" [186]. The French historian Marcel Giraud also touches on these subjects in his *Histoire de la Louisiane française* [112]. Likewise helpful in describing the French presence on the Gulf Coast is Peter J. Hamilton, *Colonial Mobile* [127]. An article important for understanding French Indian policy in Louisiana is Patricia D. Woods, "The French and the Natchez Indians in Louisiana, 1700–1731" [321]. An important new dissertation is Daniel H. Usner, Jr., "Frontier Exchange in the Lower Mississippi Valley: Race Relations and Economic Life in Colonial Louisiana, 1699–1783" [300].

No extraordinary imagination is required to accept the notion that the more peoples are present along the frontiers, the more interactions there are likely to be. This was particularly the case as the Europeans engaged in a contest for mastery in North America. The story of this struggle from 1670 until 1732 is best told by Verner W. Crane in his previously mentioned *The Southern Frontier* [66]. Whereas Crane approaches the subject from the perspective of imperial powers engaged in expansion and combat, some of the same conflicts have been analyzed from the perspective of the native peoples in two books by David Corkran: *The Creek Frontier, 1540–1783* [58] and *The Cherokee Frontier: Conflict and Survival, 1740–1762* [57]. The colonial political background for important events is analyzed by M. Eugene Sirmans in *Colonial South Carolina: A Political History, 1663–1763* [275]. While not all readers may agree with Corkran's perception of united Creek policy toward the colonial powers, his analysis of factionalism among both the Creeks and the Cherokees is useful in understanding the evolution of both tribes during the eighteenth century. Some insight into tribal rivalries is found in the anonymous "A Treaty between Virginia and the Catawbas and Cherokees, 1756" [7]. Lawrence E. Lee's *Indian Wars in North Carolina,*

1663–1763 [169] is the best work on that subject. Trade as a hingepin of war and diplomacy is not only analyzed by Crane, but also by Mary Rothrock in "Carolina Traders among the Overhill Cherokees, 1690–1760" [264].

Crane's approach and theme were taken up by John R. Alden in his *John Stuart and the Southern Colonial Frontier, 1754–1775* [6]. Alden's study is an institutional one, with emphasis on the role played by the British superintendent for Indian affairs in the South. Although he makes no attempts to analyze Indian perspectives and does not utilize French sources, this book on Stuart is helpful for analyzing the southern frontiers before the American Revolution. Also useful in this context are two studies by Philip M. Hamer: "Anglo-French Rivalry in the Cherokee Country, 1754–57" [125] and "The Wataugans and the Cherokee Indians in 1776" [126].

Given the economic and social impact of the Indian trade in the South on both sides after 1670, it is not surprising that Alden, Corkran, and Crane placed heavy emphasis on this persistent theme. Some of the trade's effect on the European community in South Carolina may be followed in Philip M. Brown, "Early Indian Trade in the Development of South Carolina: Politics, Economics, and Social Mobility during the Proprietary Period, 1670–1719" [38]. The fundamental source for much that we know not only about the Indian trade, but also about the native peoples is James Adair, *The History of the American Indians* [5]. Wilbur R.

Jacobs's discussion in *The Appalachian Indian Frontier* [8] contains a superb analysis of Edmond Atkin's colonial Indian policy and general assessment of Anglo-Indian relations. Another specific aspect of the trading environment is found in John H. Goff, "The Path to Oakfuskee" [113]. Further documentation concerning the fur trade is found in the *Journel of Colonel John Herbert* [129].

On the subject of African-Indian frontiers, primary documentation is scarce and difficult to authenticate. The researcher must be careful in accepting sources that profess to describe the unusual. John Marrant's captivity narrative describing his purported experiences among the Cherokees is a case in point. Marrant was a free Black, and his publication has been hailed as an outstanding example of Black literature. It is, to be sure, Black literature, but it is not an authentic captivity narrative. A textual analysis suggests that its model was the suffering of Jesus and that its author had had little or no contact with the Cherokees. First published in London at a time when literature about the Cherokees was popular and when Marrant was seeking to authenticate his Christian experience in order to achieve ministerial ordination, the book is largely a product of the author's imagination. A recent printing may be found in Richard Van Der Beets, *Held Captive by Indians: Selected Captivity Narratives, 1642– 1836* [189, 302].

In addition to the diversity of peoples on the southern frontiers, the reader should be aware of the space-time-place relationships in which these persons interacted. Three seminal works by historical geographers, applicable to this problem of understanding, are H. Roy Merrens, "Historical Geography and Early American History" [198]; Merrens's *Colonial North Carolina in the 18th Century: A Study in Historical Geography* [197]; and Donald W. Meinig, "American Wests: Preface to a Geographical Interpretation" [192]. Merrens's study of North Carolina is especially helpful for those seeking the forces behind the jostling of peoples on the frontiers of this colony-state and its immediate neighbors. The researcher should note his maps of European population in North Carolina, since the shadings resemble a giant plowshare aimed at the heart of the Cherokee country. Meinig's call for interdisciplinary cooperation by historians and geographers and his exemplary work suggest some of the areas where the two disciplines might benefit from joint studies of the frontier. His "The Continuous Shaping of America: A Prospectus for Geographers and Historians" [193] repeats this call for cooperation and cross-fertilization.

One historical geographer whose published and unpublished work is critical to understanding the southern frontiers is Louis De Vorsey, Jr. His *The Indian Boundary in the Southern Colonies, 1763–1775* [79] and his edited *Report of the General Survey in the Southern District of North America,* by William G. De Braham [73], are extremely useful insights into the method of European expansion onto native American tribal lands. The specific development of boundaries for two colonies may be followed in De Vorsey, "The Virginia-Cherokee Boundary of 1771" [78], and his "Indian Boundaries in Colonial Georgia" [80]. Anthropological and historical reflections on space-time-place relationships are succinctly delineated by Robin F. Wells, "Frontier Systems as a Sociocultural Type" [315]. Robert F. Berkhofer, Jr., "Space, Time, Culture and the New Frontier" [23] is an effective critique of the Turner thesis. Two recent articles focusing on cultural continuity in a southeastern region where native peoples were overrun very early are James H. Merrell, "Cultural Continuity among the Piscataway Indians of Colonial Maryland" [196], and Frank W. Porter, III, "A Century of Accommodation: The Maryland Nanticoke Indians in Colonial Maryland" [231].

Since "possession" was the rule in man-land relationships as perceived by Europeans, a great deal of attention has been paid to leading advocates of colonial expansionism such as Lord Dunmore, the last royal governor of Virginia. For strongly opposing views by historians about Dunmore as a "land-jobber" the researcher should examine Richard O. Curry's defense of Dunmore in his "Lord Dunmore—Tool of Land Jobbers?" [68] and the critique by Randolph C. Downes, "Dunmore's War: An Interpretation" [86]. Further comments critical of Dunmore but defensive of the British imperial establishment may be found in Jack M. Sosin, "The British Indian Department and

Dunmore's War" [280]. Further analysis of Virginians and land policy is found in Eugene M. Del Papa, "The Royal Proclamation of 1763" [74]. Actions of the imperial British Indian Department are elucidated in David B. Trimble, "Christopher Gist and the Indian Service in Virginia, 1757–1759" [299]. An account illustrative of Virginia's expansionism may be found in Thomas Walker's *Journal* of 1750 [307].

Hostilities at any point along the intercultural frontier tended to exacerbate or be exacerbated by tensions elsewhere. Much of what took place from the Atlantic to the Mississippi and from the Ohio to the Gulf between 1730 and 1790 was precipitated, at least in part, by European power struggles. The historian who has directed much of his attention to the frontier as a chessboard of empire is J. Leitch Wright, Jr. From his perspective, the European powers tended to shape the frontier according to their needs and ambitions. Wright has explored this thesis at length in *Anglo-Spanish Rivalry in North America* [325] and in *Britain and the American Frontier, 1783–1815* [328]. Specific studies of shifting settlement patterns precipitated by European intrusions are Jacqueline K. Voorges, "The Attakapas Post: The First Acadian Settlement" [305] and Barton J. Starr, "Campbell Town: French Huguenots in British West Florida" [283].

Since Georgia lay exposed to attack and invasion from any or all of three sides, the British government was forced to give a good deal of attention to that point on her global frontiers. Basic to an understanding of

Georgia's official policy is William W. Abbott, *The Royal Governors of Georgia, 1754–1775* [1]. The general views provided by Wright and Abbott might be supplemented for the student of Georgia affairs by reading Larry Ivers's military-history oriented *British Drums on the Southern Frontier* [147] and two somewhat more balanced articles by Trevor R. Reese: "Georgia in Anglo-Spanish Diplomacy, 1736–1739" [251] and "Britain's Military Support of Georgia in the War of 1739–1748" [252]. For commentary about Georgia's Indian affairs during the period, the researcher should consult John P. Corry, *Indian Affairs in Georgia, 1732–1756* [59]. The multiethnic nature of early Georgia society is also reflected in Fussell Chalker, "Highland Scots in the Georgia Lowlands" [49]. A more recent study dealing with the Georgia Indian frontiers in the mid-eighteenth century is Corkran, *The Creek Frontier* [58]. Since Corkran begins his discussion of Georgia's first frontier with the negotiation between Oglethorpe and the Yamacraws, then carries the story forward as part of his larger examination of the Creeks, his book is far more useful than Corry's.

Georgia's next neighbor northward had enjoyed a prosperous domination of the southern Indian trade for more than half a century before Georgia was founded. Two books previously mentioned provide information basic to understanding South Carolina's frontier with the native peoples: Crane, *The Southern Frontier* [66], and Alden, *John Stuart* [6]. For the colonial, rather than the imperial, view, publications of possible use that might be described as "limited colony studies" are Robert I. Meriwether, *The Expansion of South Carolina, 1729–1765* [195]; Robert W. Ramsay, *Carolina Cradle* [250]; and Chapman J. Milling, *Red Carolinians* [203]. A significant collection of documents pertaining to the South Carolina frontier was edited by William L. McDowell, Jr., as *The Colonial Records of South Carolina: Documents Relating to Indian Affairs, 1754–1765* [182]. These published documents and the other "Indian books" at the South Carolina Archives are a treasurehouse for insight into the frontier before the American Revolution.

Whenever the winds of war blew across the homelands of the imperial powers, the colonies and frontiers in North America were also involved. Activities on the southern frontiers before the American Revolution are a part of the discussions in the works on Dunmore's War and the boundary with the southern Indians that were mentioned above. Another imperialist interpretation of the frontier has been published by Jack Sosin in his *The Revolutionary Frontier* [281]. Because of the author's totally White-centered and institutional orientation, many readers may not find the study as useful for its interpretation as for its comprehensiveness and bibliography. An older, but still useful study of shifting areas of empire is Charles L. Mowat, *East Florida as a British Province* [209].

Angry Seas: The American Revolution and Early National Period

The southern frontier during the American Revolution has been approached by a number of authors in different ways. In addition to James Adair's 1775 *History* [5], the best contemporary reflection of the revolutionary frontier and its impact upon all peoples of the region is found in the writings of William Bartram [17, 18, 19], who traveled extensively throughout the southern colonies from the 1770s through the 1790s. *The Southern Indians in the American Revolution* [216], by James H. O'Donnell, III, is a rather narrow, White-centered examination of British efforts to engage and American efforts to keep neutral the major southern Indian tribes. Two more recent studies by the same author dealing with two specific states and the Indians make an effort at a more balanced view by at least recognizing the native peoples as functioning entities. These are *The Georgia Indian Frontier, 1773–1783* [217] and *The Cherokees of North Carolina in the American Revolution* [218]. North Carolina's Cherokee difficulties have also been examined by Robert L. Ganyard in his "Threat from the West: North Carolina and the Cherokee, 1776–1778" [106]. James H. O'Donnell has also dealt briefly with one of the major native American leaders to emerge on the southern frontier during the war: "Alexander McGillivray: Training for Leadership, 1777–1783" [215]. Michael D. Green's recent biographical study of McGillivray should also be consulted [118].

Another person who made his presence felt on the frontier during the war was Thomas Brown. His wartime exploits have been chronicled by Gary D. Olson in "Loyalists and the American Revolution: Thomas Brown and the South Carolina Backcountry, 1775–1776" [219] and "Thomas Brown, Loyalist Partisan, and the Revolutionary War in Georgia, 1778–1782" [220]. The consideration given to native Americans in overall British planning may be followed in Paul H. Smith, *Loyalists and Redcoats* [278].

Even as the Revolution was being fought, the native peoples faced new onslaughts of settlers moving west. Since the Cherokees had been crushed in the Cherokee War of 1776, boatloads of settlers (some not without mishap) bypassed the Cherokee towns by sailing down the Tennessee River and thence ascending the Cumberland to develop a new settlement at Nashville. Brief accounts of this intrusion into lands the native Americans assumed were theirs may be found in Katherine R. Barnes, "Robertson's Journey to Nashville" [15] and Anita A. Goodstein, "Leadership on the Nashville Frontier" [115]. Early Tennessee is also chronicled by Thomas P. Abernathy in *From Frontier to Plantation in Tennessee* [3].

Since France had officially withdrawn from North America following the settlement at Paris in 1763, Spain was the only rival left to challenge Britain's hegemony. Essential documents about Spanish activities in the Southeast during this period are available in Manuel Serrano y Sanz, *España y los Indios Cherokis y*

Chactas en la segunda mital del siglo XVIII [271]. Although Spain did not wish to jeopardize her own position as a colonial power by becoming involved in the war between Great Britain and the United States, she would seek to use the conflict to her advantage, if she could do so without weakening herself. An older study that remains acceptable as an overall account of Spain on the southern frontiers is John W. Caughey, *Bernardo de Galvez in Louisiana, 1776–1783* [46]. British resistance to Spanish control is described in Caughey's "The Natchez Rebellion of 1781 and Its Aftermath" [45]. Two specific studies of Spain's northeastern frontier by Caughey that are useful for their source materials are *McGillivray of the Creeks* [47] and *East Florida, 1783–1785* [48]. Caughey's works may be supplemented with Eric Beerman, "José de Ezpeleta: Alabama's First Spanish Commandant during the American Revolution" [21], and Gilbert C. Din, "Protecting the 'Barrera': Spain's Defenses in Louisiana, 1763–1779 [83]. An account of Florida as a British outpost of empire is Cecil Johnson, *British West Florida, 1763–1783* [149].

The modern scholar who has written extensively on Spain's northeast Gulf frontiers is Jack D. L. Holmes. Four titles published by Holmes that may be useful to students of southeastern frontiers are *Gayoso* [134]; "Spanish Policy toward the Southern Indians in the 1790's" [138]; "Spanish Treaties with the West Florida Indians, 1784–1802" [136]; and "Up the Tombigbee with the Spaniards: Juan de la Villebeuvre and the Treaty of Boucfouca (1793)" [139].

Spain's borderlands on the Gulf Coast were a multiethnic frontier where there was a constant movement of peoples, a theme well developed by Wright, Caughey, and Holmes. Because of Spain's insistence on control of immigration and documentation of mixed-bloods, several scholars have been able to carry out fruitful research in those areas. Anthropologist Kathleen A. Deagan has explored the question of "Mestizaje in Colonial Saint Augustine" [70], and historian Gilbert C. Sin has focused on immigration policy in his "Immigration Policy of Esteban Miro" [81] and "Spain's Immigration Policy and Efforts in Louisiana during the American Revolution" [82]. One particularly revealing episode for the student of southern frontiers is followed by Robert L. Gold in his discussion of the transfer of peoples across the Gulf in "The Settlement of the Pensacola Indians in New Spain, 1763–1770" [114]. Also useful is David H. White, "The Indian Policy of Juan Vicente Folch, Governor of Spanish Mobile, 1781–1792" [317].

If Spain wished to regulate immigration and document mixed-bloods, she no less wanted trade and commerce under her watchful eye. When she took over the Floridas in 1784 she was confronted with an Indian trade monopolized by the English company of Panton, Leslie, and Company, whose representatives operated as far away as the present Memphis, and whose influence in general was furthered by the portion of the company assigned to the mixed-blood Creek leader Alexander McGillivray. Two older studies about

McGillivray by Caughey [47] and O'Donnell [215] offer some insight into McGillivray's activities on behalf of himself, his tribe, and the company. Two recent articles by Thomas D. Watson offer insight into the company itself and its operations both in the name of and under the protection of Spain: "Continuity in Commerce: Development of the Panton, Leslie, and Company Trade Monopoly in West Florida" [313] and "A Scheme Gone Awry: Bernardo de Galvez, Gilberto Antonio de Maxent, and the Southern Indian Trade" [314]. McGillivray's interaction with his Spanish allies is nicely analyzed in Caroline M. Burson, *Stewardship of Don Esteban Miro* [39].

Adventurers were not uncommon in a volatile frontier situation, and it is no surprise that one of the flies in the Hispano-Indian ointment was an American Loyalist named William A. Bowles. The standard work on his life is by that prolific student of the frontier, J. Leitch Wright, Jr. [324]. Bowles's capacity for braggadocio and Wright's acceptance of his subject's assessments has led anthropologist William C. Sturtevant to raise some questions about Wright's lack of criticism of Bowles's accounts in "The Cherokee Frontiers, the French Revolution, and William Augustus Bowles" [288]. Another recent look at Bowles's filibustering career was taken by David H. White in "The Spaniards and William Augustus Bowles in Florida, 1799–1803" [318].

After the close of the American Revolution there was a great rush for power among the interests on the southern frontiers. The tribes, the federal government of the newly independent nation, the governments of the several states, Spanish authorities, land speculators, and merchants looked upon the change in control as an opportunity for profit, themes the researcher will find in appropriate volumes of *The Territorial Papers of the United States* [44], edited by Clarence Carter. The volumes on Alabama (18), Arkansas (19–21), Florida (22–26), and Mississippi (5–6) are of special importance. Since the federal and state governments regarded themselves as winners and the native peoples as losers (with land being the spoils), most of the tribes worked feverishly to protect themselves against a new onslaught of expansionism. Resistance, diplomacy, and accommodation, or combinations thereof, were the strategies adopted by most of the tribal peoples.

Alexander McGillivray's diplomatic balancing act between 1783 and 1790 must be pieced together from a number of sources. The older Caughey work [47] and also Merritt B. Pound, *Benjamin Hawkins: Indian Agent* [239], contain some useful information, but they should be augmented by some of the more recent essays on the Creeks. Corkran's *The Creek Frontier* [58] is useful, as are two other works: Clyde R. Ferguson, "Andrew Pickens and United States Policy toward the Creek Nation" [95]; and Mary Jane McDaniel, "Relations between the Creek Indians, Georgia, and the United States, 1783–1797" [180]. Ferguson further comments on Creek leadership difficulties after McGillivray's death in his "Confrontation at Coleraine" [96].

After the revolution in France, the machinations of *les citoyens* reached to the southern frontiers, a story told by Richard K. Murdoch in *The Georgia-Florida Frontier, 1793–1796: Spanish Reaction to French Intrigue and American Designs* [210]. Some of the same material was covered generally in an older work by Arthur P. Whitaker, *The Spanish American Frontier, 1783–1795* [316]. Also helpful in reaching an understanding of the Hispano-Franco-Indian frontiers is a dissertation by Peter Zahendra, "Spanish West Florida, 1781–1821" [335]. One of the French schemers on the southern frontier during this period was Louis L. de Milfort. Since his personality and methods were similar to those of Bowles, great care must be exercised in taking him at his word. For those interested in examining his account of life among the Creeks, see his *Memoirs; or, A Cursory Glance at My Various Travels and My Sojourn in the Creek Nation* [202]. One of several British colonials trying to live on the same frontier is described in V. Haynes Robert's "Life on the Mississippi Frontier, 1776–1780: Case of Matthew Phelps" [256].

Among the land speculators casting a jealous eye on the acreage of the South was a group headed by William Blount. Blount's biography by William H. Masterson [190] is helpful in unraveling this scheme, as are the documents in *The John Gray Blount Papers* [156], edited by Alice B. Keith. For an overall picture of western land schemers after the American Revolution, useful surveys are contained in two books by Thomas P. Abernathy: *Western Lands and the American Revolution* [2] and *The South in the New Nation* [4]. A document dealing specifically with Virginia's pressure on the Chickasaws is Robert S. Cotterill, "The Virginia-Chickasaw Treaty of 1783" [60].

In the two decades after the American Revolution, the jostling of peoples continued on the southern frontiers. Traditional accounts from the White perspective are found in Randolph C. Downes, "Cherokee-American Relations in the Upper Tennessee Valley, 1776–1791" [87], and his "Creek-American Relations, 1790–1795" [88]. Within the native societies the constant pressure from the Europeans produced changes in tribal location and life-styles. As an introduction to understanding the enormous adjustments ultimately made by native peoples of the region, one should read Fred Gearing's *Priests and Warriors* [108], which focuses on the the Cherokees. The author's reconstruction of Cherokee village structures gives greater significance to the kinds of changes that tribe was to undergo. As a complement to Gearing the researcher should consult two provocative works by John P. Reid on the development of Cherokee tribal law: *A Law of Blood: The Primitive Law of the Cherokee People* [253] and *A Better Kind of Hatchet: Law, Trade, and Diplomacy in the Cherokee Nation during the Early Years of European Contact* [254]. Another study crucial to an understanding of this subject is Rennard Strickland's *Fire and the Spirits: Cherokee Law from Clan to Court* [285]. Although Strickland's emphasis is more on the evolution of Cherokee jurisprudence in the nineteenth century, the early chapters do touch the late eighteenth century. Another influence on evolving Cherokee life is traced by Rennard Strickland in "Christian Gottlieb Priber: Utopian Precursor of the Cherokee Government" [284]. Gary C. Goodwin, *Cherokees in Transition* [116] is an excellent discussion of the interrelationship of culture change and environment prior to 1775.

Among the changes that took place in native American societies between 1783 and 1810 was the gradual introduction of the practice of holding Blacks as slaves. The best recent book on the Cherokee practice of slavery is Theda Perdue, *Slavery and the Evolution of Cherokee Society* [229]. Richard Halliburton's *Red over Black* [123] is less successful in affording an understanding of the subject. With respect to the question of slavery among the Creeks, there is no work that compares favorably to Perdue. Daniel Littlefield's recent *Africans and Creeks* [174] attempts to survey documented instances of the presence of Africans in Creek society from 1540 to 1870, but in the end the reader may conclude he knows neither Creeks nor Africans.

The angry waves of war and its aftermath, which produced such internal stress as noted by Gearing and external destruction as suggested by O'Donnell, also provided the milieu out of which arose the individuals who would come to hold positions of leadership among native American groups in the next generations. If one wishes to speculate on some common traits, it appears that the new leaders would at least in part come from among the "mixed-bloods" who combined traditional

tribal leadership patterns with the entrepreneurial attitudes held by European frontier leaders. One of the
earliest and most successful of these post-Revolutionary
leaders was Alexander McGillivray, who has been
mentioned previously.

Within the last decade scholars have turned to biographical foci in order to write "Indian history." The
task of making these examinations Indian-centered is
the Herculean labor where many fail. In W. David
Baird's *Peter Pitchlynn* [10], for example, there is much
of Pitchlynn as entrepreneur and little about emergent
Choctaw leadership. A more successful venture in this
field is Gary E. Moulton's *John Ross* [208], which incor-
porates both Ross's life and the larger story of the an-
guish suffered by all the Cherokee people during the
period of removal.

Removal

The literature of removal is voluminous in quantity
and uneven in quality. Of some use in understanding
the background of removal is Bernard Sheehan's *Seeds
of Extinction* [273]. Although Sheehan always assumes a
White-centered initiative, thereby belittling Indian sov-
ereignty and intelligence, he has contributed toward
our understanding of Jeffersonian intellectual perceptions of the Indian. Equally requisite to an understanding of the social forces at work in the drive for removal
is Robert F. Berkhofer, Jr., *Salvation and the Savage: An*

Analysis of Protestant Missions and American Indian Response, 1781–1862 [24].

The older but still acceptable general account of removal is Grant Foreman, *Indian Removal: The Emigration of the Five Civilized Tribes of Indians* [100]. Although many works on removal fall into a genre most aptly described as "trail of tears" narratives, there are attempts to assess the story from a less emotional viewpoint. The experiences of the Cherokees have been scrutinized from several perspectives in essays such as Mary E. Young, "Indian Removal and the Attack on Tribal Autonomy: The Cherokee Case" [334]; William G. McLaughlin and Walter H. Conser, Jr., "The Cherokees in Transition: A Statistical Analysis of the Federal Cherokee Census of 1835" [184]; Oliver Knight, "Cherokee Society under the Stress of Removal, 1820–1846" [162]; and Walter H. Conser, Jr., "John Ross and the Cherokee Resistance Campaign, 1833–1838" [54]. One should also refer to Moulton's biography of Ross [208] for additional commentary on the Cherokees and removal. The best one-volume account of the struggles burdening the Choctaws is by Arthur H. DeRosier, *The Removal of the Choctaw Indians* [77]. The same author has traced the intricacies and chicanery of removal negotiations in "Negotiations for the Removal of the Choctaws" [75] and "Andrew Jackson and Negotiations for the Removal of the Choctaw Indians" [76]. The Creek difficulties were recounted by Mary E. Young in "The Creek Frauds: A Study in Conscience and Corruption" [331]. The most recent study about federal policy toward the Creeks, though weak on the Creeks themselves, is Michael D. Green, "Federal-State Conflict in the Administration of Indian Policy: Georgia, Alabama, and the Creeks, 1824–1834" [117]. Two essays on Creek removal by Richard Hryneiwici are "The Creek Treaty of Washington, 1826" [142] and "The Creek Treaty of November 15, 1827" [143]. Removal itself is chronicled in the moving account "The Journal of a Party of Emigrating Creek Indians, 1835–1836" [175], by Gaston Litton.

For a comparison of the Creek, Choctaw, and Chickasaw problems in this period, the most useful study is Mary E. Young, *Redskins, Ruffleshirts, and Rednecks: Indian Allotments in Alabama and Mississippi, 1830–1860* [332]. Young's analysis of the removal "problem" in general as well as of the clash between Jacksonian conscience and economic materialism is brilliantly put forward both in her *Redskins* and in "Indian Removal and Land Allotment: The Civilized Tribes and Jacksonian Justice" [333].

The serious student of removal and its impact also will wish to consider the context within which removal policy was developed and implemented by reading Reginald Horsman, "American Indian Policy and the Origins of Manifest Destiny" [141], and Wilcomb E. Washburn, "Indian Removal Policy: Administrative, Historical and Moral Criteria for Judging Its Success or Failure" [312].

Within the last decade the direction of research on the removal era has absorbed at least one rather radical twist. Historians and other academics seeking to apply

Eriksonian and Freudian psychohistorical methods have braved the depths of Andrew Jackson's ocean. One such daring adventurer was Michael P. Rogin in *Fathers and Children: Andrew Jackson and the Subjugation of the American Indian* [260]. While some may accept the validity of psychohistory as *one* tool, Rogin's Freudianism goes too far. Anyone familiar with the conventional symbolism of familial rhetoric used by native peoples long before the arrival of the Europeans will be unable to accept Rogin. Much of the discussion about deterministic interpretations of Jacksonian policy toward native peoples has been reviewed by Martin H. Quitt in his "Jackson, Indians, and Psychohistory: A Review Essay" [249].

Additional perspectives on the political, economic, and social context of removal may be gained by consulting the literature of reappraisal concerning Jacksonian policy toward removal. Francis Paul Prucha's challenging article of a decade ago, in the fashion of the "needs and opportunities for study" approach, "Andrew Jackson's Indian Policy: A Reassessment" [242] has been answered in part by Ronald N. Satz in *American Indian Policy in the Jacksonian Era* [268]. However, Prucha's call for more research into Indian affairs during the Jacksonian period and Satz's response were given no notice by Ronald P. Formisano in his "Toward a Reorientation of Jacksonian Politics: A Review of the Literature, 1959–1975" [102].

In any consideration of the peoples on the southeastern frontiers, there is always the problem of inadequate information on specific tribal groups or incidents in their histories. A good overview is still available in Robert S. Cotterill, *The Southern Indians: The Story of the Civilized Tribes before Removal* [61]. When such is the case, the only recourse may be to tribal studies. With regard to the Chickasaws, for example, the reader's starting point must be Arrell M. Gibson, *The Chickasaws* [110]. Gibson opens his narrative with an extremely useful ethnohistorical essay and then follows the Chickasaws as a people living in their historic homelands on the east bank of the Mississippi through their removal across the great river into Indian Territory and onward to their eventual dissolution as a "nation" in 1906.

In the case of the Chickasaws it is appropriate to return again to the question of mixed-blood leadership after the American Revolution, a matter mentioned earlier. One of the prominent "mixed-blood" families among the Chickasaws has been studied by Gary B. Braden in "The Colberts and the Chickasaw Nation" [34]. It is useful to examine the interface created by the presence of the Colberts, whose father was a British Indian agent, in order to understand how traders and imperial agents gained the position and influence they would pass on to their mixed-blood descendants to perpetuate through several generations and across the Mississippi into Indian Territory.

Among the Choctaws, moreover, "mixed bloods" also came to grasp major portions of power. Despite the emphasis on Peter Pitchlynn as entrepreneur, Baird's recent study of that leader [10] underlines the prominence of "mixed-bloods" in Choctaw leadership. The same theme is a part of Arthur DeRosier's study. A guide to the larger problems encountered by the Choctaws is Angie Debo, *the Rise and Fall of the Choctaw Republic* [72]. Two articles that shed light on the Choctaws at particularly crucial time periods are Jack D. L. Holmes, "The Choctaws in 1795" [135], and Jon A. Schlenker, "An Historical Analysis of the Family Life of the Choctaw Indians" [270]. Schlenker and Jesse O. McKee have recently contributed a useful synthesis that focuses on cultural geography, published as *The Choctaws: Cultural Evolution of a Native American Tribe* [183].

For those further interested in the Creeks, first reference should be to Michael D. Green, *The Creeks: A Critical Bibliography* [119]. Green offers the most up-to-date and thorough review of the information about the Creeks that a reader could desire. Much of the early Hispano-Creek, Franco-Creek, Anglo-Creek, and African-Creek story has been chronicled by Corkran in his *The Creek Frontier* [58]. There are also appropriate sections on the Creeks in Hudson's *The Southeastern Indians* [145] and Grant Foreman's *The Five Civilized Tribes* [101]. Given the attention to war with the Creeks during the Jacksonian period, it might be well also to consult the standard nineteenth-century chronicle of that struggle, written by H. S. Halbert and T. H. Ball, *The Creek War of 1813 and 1814* [122]. Halbert and Ball should be supplemented with Ross Hassig, "Internal Conflict in the Creek War of 1813–1814" [128], and

Kenneth L. Valliere, "The Creek War of 1836: A Military History" [301].

For information about those Creeks who became Seminoles, the older general work is Edwin C. McReynolds, *The Seminoles* [185]. Since the publication of McReynolds's work there have been several important analyses of Seminole adaptation to external as well as internal pressures. A general historical treatment of Seminole Creek migration was offered by James W. Covington in "Migration of the Seminoles into Florida, 1700–1820" [62]. For aspects of cultural change, however, one should consult Charles Fairbanks, "The Ethno-Archaeology of the Florida Seminoles" [92]. As a complement to Fairbanks's work one should also inspect an essay by Alan K. Craig and Christopher S. Peebles, "Ethnoecologic Change among the Seminoles: 1740–1840" [65]. Likewise useful in this connection is William C. Sturtevant's "Creek into Seminole" [287].

A significant aspect of Seminole life was the tribe's continuing interaction with Blacks who took up residence with them. Kenneth W. Porter's several articles on this subject are helpful. These include "Florida Slaves and Free Negroes in the Seminole War" [234]; "Negroes and the East Florida Annexation Plot, 1811–1813" [235]; and "Negroes and the Seminole War" [237].

On the Cherokees, the reader is fortunate to have Raymond D. Fogelson's *The Cherokees: A Critical Bibliography* [97]. This is a thorough review of the literature on this important tribe, and anyone interested in doing serious reading on the Cherokees should consult it first. Three older general accounts that may be referred to are John P. Brown, *Old Frontiers* [37]; Marion Starkey, *The Cherokee Nation* [282]; and Grace Woodward, *The Cherokees* [322]. Of limited usefulness but nevertheless having some merit is Henry T. Malone, *Cherokees of the Old South* [188]. Since both James Mooney, "Myths of the Cherokees" [204], and Charles C. Royce, *The Cherokee Nation of Indians* [266], have recently been reprinted, the interested reader may consult these older, but still useful, works. Among prerequisite recent essays is Theda Perdue's challenging interpretation, "Rising from the Ashes: The Cherokee Phoenix as an Ethnohistorical Source" [228].

ALPHABETICAL LIST AND INDEX

*Denotes items suitable for secondary school students

Item

No.

Essay

Page

No.

[1]   Abbott, William W. 1959. *The Royal Governors of Georgia, 1754–1775.* Chapel Hill: University of North Carolina Press.   (39)

[2]   Abernathy, Thomas P. 1937. *Western Lands and the American Revolution.* New York: D. Appleton-Century.   (47)

[3]   ———. 1955. *From Frontier to Plantation in Tennessee.* Memphis: Memphis State University Press.   (42)

[4]   ———. 1961. *The South in the New Nation.* Baton Rouge: Louisiana State University Press.   (48)

[5]   Adair, James. 1775. *The History of the American Indians: Particularly Those Adjoining to the Mississippi, East and West Florida, Georgia, South and North Carolina and Virginia.* London: E. C. Dilly. Re-

printed, Johnson City, Tenn.: Watauga
Press, 1930.   (34, 41)

[6]   Alden, John R. 1944. *John Stuart and the
Southern Colonial Frontier, 1754–1755.*
Ann Arbor: University of Michigan
Press. Reprinted, New York: Gordian
Press, 1966.   (34, 39)

[7]   Anonymous. 1906. "A Treaty between
Virginia and the Catawbas and
Cherokees, 1756." *Virginia Magazine of
History and Biography* 13:225–64.   (33)

[8]   Atkin, Edmond. [1775] 1967. *The Appalachian Indian Frontier: The Edmond
Atkin Report and Plan of 1775*, ed. Wilbur R. Jacobs. Lincoln: University of
Nebraska Press.   (35)

[9]   Bailyn, Bernard. 1959. "Politics and
Social Structure in Colonial Virginia."
In *Seventeenth-Century America, ed.* James
M. Smith. Chapel Hill: University of
North Carolina Press.   (23)

[10] Baird, W. Daivd. 1972. *Peter Pitchlynn:
Chief of the Choctaws.* Norman: University of Oklahoma Press.   (50, 54)

[11] Bannon, John Francis. 1970. *The Spanish Borderlands Frontier, 1513–1821.* New York: Holt, Rinehart and Winston. Available through University of New Mexico Press.   (15)

[12] Barbour, Philip L. 1964. *The Three Worlds of Captain John Smith.* Boston: Houghton Mifflin.   (22)

[13] ———. 1970. *Pocahontas and Her World.* Boston: Houghton Mifflin.   (22)

[14] Barcia Carballido y Zuñiga, Andrés González de. 1723. *Ensayo cronológico para la historia general de la Florida.* Madrid: En la Oficina real, y à costa de N. Rodriguez Franco. New ed. published as *Barcia's Chronological History of the Continent of Florida,* trans. Anthony Kerrigan. Gainesville: University of Florida Press, 1951. Reprinted, Westport, Conn.: Greenwood, 1970.   (12)

[15] Barnes, Katherine R. 1976. "Robertson's Journey to Nashville. . . ." *Tennessee Historical Quarterly* 35:145–61.   (42)

[16] Barrientos, Bartolomé. 1965. [1568] *Pedro Menéndez de Avilés, Founder of*

Florida. Translated by Anthony Kerrigan. Gainesville: University of Florida Press. Also see [107] for the Spanish edition.   (11)

[17]   Bartram, William. 1773–74. "Travels in Georgia and Florida, 1773–74: A Report to Doctor John Fothergill." *Transactions of the American Philosophical Society,* n.s., 33, part 2 (1943):121–242.   (41)

[18]   ———. 1789. "Observations on the Creek and Cherokee Indians." With prefatory and supplementary notes by E. G. Squier. *Transactions of the American Ethnological Society* 3, part 1 (1853):1–81.   (41)

[19]   ———. 1791. *Travels through North and South Carolina, Georgia, East and West Florida, the Cherokee Country, the Extensive Territories of the Muscogulges or Creek Confederacy, and the Country of the Choctaws. Containing an Account of the Soil and Natural Production of Those Regions; Together with Observations on the Manners of the Indians.* Philadelphia: James and Johnson. Reprinted as *Travels of William Bartram,* ed. Mark Van Doren, New York: Dover 1928. New ed. in facsimile,

New York: Barnes and Noble, 1940.
New ed., ed. Francis Harper, New Haven: Yale University Press, 1958.   (41)

[20] Beckwith, Ian. 1976. "Captain John
      Smith: The Yeoman Background." *His-
      tory Today* 26:444–51.   (22)

[21] Beerman, Eric. 1976. "José de Ezpeleta:
      Alabama's First Spanish Commandant
      during the American Revolution." *Ala-
      bama Review* 29:249–60.   (43)

[22] Bennett, Charles E., ed. 1964. *Laudon-
      nière and Fort Caroline: History and Doc-
      uments*. Gainesville: University of
      Florida Press.   (10)

[23] Berkhofer, Robert F., Jr. 1964. "Space,
      Time, Culture and the New Frontier."
      Agricultural History 38:21–30.   (37)

[24] ———. 1965. *Salvation and the Savage:
      An Analysis of Protestant Missions and
      American Indian Response, 1781–1862*.
      Lexington: University of Kentucky
      Press.   (51)

[25] Bolton, Herbert Eugene. 1917. "The
      Mission as a Frontier Institution in the

Spanish-American Colonies." *American Historical Review* 23:42–61.   (15)

[26]   ———. 1925. "Spanish Resistance to Carolina Traders in Western Georgia, 1608–1704." *Georgia Historical Quarterly* 9:115–30.   (30)

[27]   Bolton, Herbert E., and Mary Ross. 1925. *The Debatable Land: A Sketch of the Anglo-Spanish Contest for the Georgia Country.* Berkeley: University of California Press.   (30)

[28]   Bonnefoy, Antoine. 1928. [1741–42] "Journal of Antoine Bonnefoy." In *Early Travels in the Tennessee Country, 1540–1800,* with introduction, annotations, and index by Samuel Cole Williams, pp. 147–64. Johnson City, Tenn.: Watauga Press.   (32)

[29]   Bourne, Edward Gaylord, ed. 1904. *Narratives of the Career of Hernando de Soto in the Conquest of Florida as Told by a Knight of Elvas and in a Relation by Luys Hernández de Biedma, Factor of the Expedition, Translated by Buckingham Smith Together with an Account of De Soto's Expedition Based on the Diary of Rodrigo Ranjel,*

His Private Secretary, Translated from Oviedo's Historia General y Natural de las Indias. 2 vols. New York: A. S. Barnes.   (x, 6)

[30]   Boyd, Mark F. 1937. "Expedition of Marcus Delgado from Apalache to the Upper Creek Country in 1686." *Florida Historical Quarterly* 16–17:3–32.   (17)

[31]   ———. 1939. "Mission Sites in Florida." *Florida Historical Quarterly* 17:255.   (17)

[32]   ———., ed. 1953. "Further Consideration of the Apalachee Missions." *Americas* 9:459–79.   (17)

[33]   Boyd, Mark F., Hale G. Smith, and John W. Griffin. 1951. *Here They Once Stood: The Tragic End of the Apalachee Missions.* Gainesville: University of Florida Press.   (17)

[34]   Braden, Gary B. 1958. "The Colberts and the Chickasaw Nation." *Tennessee Historical Quarterly* 17:222–49, 318–35.   (54)

[35]   Brain, Jeffrey P., Alan Toth, and Antonio Rodriguez-Buckingham. 1974. "Ethnohistoric Archaeology and the Desoto Entrada into the Lower

Mississippi Valley." In *The Conference on Historic Site Archaeology Papers*, 7(1972):232-89. Columbia: Institute of Archaeology and Anthropology, University of South Carolina.   (8)

[36] Brebner, John B. 1933. *Explorers of North America —1492-1806*. London: A. C. Bleck. Reprinted, Cleveland: World, 1964.   (3)

[37] Brown, John P. 1938. *Old Frontiers*. Kingsport, Tenn.: Kingsport Press.   (57)

[38] Brown, Phillip M. 1975. "Early Indian Trade in the Development of South Carolina: Politics, Economics, and Social Mobility during the Proprietary Period, 1670-1719." *South Carolina Historical Magazine* 76:118-28.   (34)

[39] Burson, Caroline M. 1924. *Stewardship of Don Esteban Miro*. New Orleans: American Printing Company.   (45)

[40] Bushnell, David I. 1927. *Drawings by A. DeBatz in Louisiana, 1732-1735*. Smithsonien *Micellaneous Collections* 80(5). Reprinted, Ann Arbor: University of Michigan Press, 1979.   (20, 32)

[41]   ———. 1927. "John White—the First
English Artist to Visit America, 1585."
*Virginia Magazine of History and Biog-
raphy* 35:419–30; 36:17–26, 124–34.   (19)

[42]   Caldwell, Norman W. 1938. "Chicksaw
Threat to French Control of the
Mississippi in the 1740's." *Chronicles of
Oklahoma* 16:465–92.   (32)

[43]   Canny, Nicholas. 1979. "The Permissive Frontier: The Problem of Social
Control in English Settlements in Ireland and Virginia, 1550–1660." In *The
Westward Enterprise: English Activities in
Ireland, the Atlantic and America, 1480–
1650*, ed. K. R. Andrews, N. P. Canny,
and P. E. H. Hair, pp. 17–44. Detroit:
Wayne State University Press.   (23)

[44]   Carter, Clarence. 1934–62. *The Territorial Papers of the United States.* Washington, D.C.: Government Printing Office.
See vols. 5–6, 18–26.   (46)

[45]   Caughey, John W. 1933. "The Natchez
Rebellion of 1781 and Its Aftermath."
Louisiana Historical Quarterly 16:57–83.   (43)

[46] ———. 1934. *Bernardo de Galvez in Louisiana, 1776–1783.* Berkeley: University of California Press. (43)

*[47] ———. 1938 *McGillivray of the Creeks.* Norman: University of Oklahoma Press. (43, 45, 46)

[48] ———. 1949. *East Florida, 1783–85: A File of Documents Assembled and Many of Them Translated by Joseph Byrne Lockey.* Berkeley: University of California Press. (43)

[49] Chalker, Fussell. 1976. "Highland Scots in the Georgia Lowlands." *Georgia Historical Quarterly* 60: 35–42. (39)

[50] Champigny, Jean, Chevalier de. 1774. *The Present State of the Country and Inhabitants, Europeans, and Indians, of Louisiana.* London: J. Millam. (32)

[51] Chatelain, Verne E. 1941. *The Defenses of Spanish Florida, 1565–1763.* Washington, D.C.: Carnegie Institution of Washington. (13)

[52] Chiappelli, Fredi, ed. 1976. *First Images of America: The Impact of the New World*

on the Old. 2 vols. Berkeley: University
of California Press.   (20)

[53]   Connor, Jeanette, ed. and trans.
       1925–30. *Colonial Records of Spanish
       Florida: Letters and Reports of Governors
       and Secular Persons, 1570–1580.* 2 vols.
       Deland: Florida State Historical Society. (14)

[54]   Conser, Walter H., Jr. 1978. "John Ross
       and the Cherokee Resistance Cam-
       paign, 1833–1838." *Journal of Southern
       History* 44:91–212.   (51)

[55]   Corbitt, Duvon, trans and ed. 1936–41.
       "Papers Relating to the Georgia-Florida
       Frontier, 1784–1800." *Georgia Historical
       Quarterly* 20:356–65; 21:73–83, 185–
       88, 274–93, 373–81; 22:72–76, 184–
       91, 286–91, 391–94; 23:77–79, 189–
       202, 300–303, 381–87; 24:77–83,
       150–57, 257–71, 374–81; 25:67–76,
       159–71.   (18)

[56]   ———. 1937–1938. "Papers from the
       Spanish Archives Relating to Tennessee
       and the Old Southwest, 1783–1800."
       *East Tennessee Historical Society Publica-
       tions* 9:44.   (18)

[57]   Corkran, David. 1962. *The Cherokee Frontier: Conflict and Survival, 1740–1762.* Norman: University of Oklahoma Press.   (33)

[58]   ———. 1967. *The Creek Frontier, 1540–1783.* Norman: University of Oklahoma Press.   (33, 39, 46, 55)

[59]   Corry, John Pitts. 1936. *Indian Affairs in Georgia, 1732–1756.* Philadelphia: University of Pennsylvania Press.   (39)

[60]   Cotterill, Robert S. 1942. "The Virginia-Chickasaw Treaty of 1783." *Journal of Southern History* 8:482–96.   (48)

[61]   ———. 1954. *The Southern Indians: The Story of the Civilized Tribes before Removal.* Norman: University of Oklahoma Press.   (54)

[62]   Covington, James W. 1968. "Migration of the Seminoles into Florida, 1700–1820." *Florida Historical Quarterly* 46:340–57.   (56)

[63]   ———. 1972. "Apalachee Indians, 1704–1763." *Florida Historical Quarterly* 50:366–84.   (17)

[64]   ———. 1975. "Relations between the Eastern Timucuan Indians and the French and Spanish, 1564–1567." In *Four Centuries of Southern Indians,* ed. Charles Hudson, pp. 11–27. Athens: University of Georgia Press.   (10, 13)

[65]   Craig, Alan K., and Christopher S. Peebles. 1974. "Ethnoecologic Change among the Seminoles, 1740–1840." In *Man and Cultural Heritage: Essays in Honor of Fred B. Kniffen,* ed. H. J. Walker and William G. Haag. Vol. 5 of *Geoscience and Man,* gen. ed. Bob Perkins. Baton Rouge: Louisiana State University for the Department of Geology.   (56)

*[66]   Crane, Verner W. 1929. *The Southern Frontier, 1670–1732.* Durham, N.C.: Duke University Press.   (30, 33, 39)

[67]   Craven, Wesley F. 1944. "Indian Policy in Early Virginia." *William and Mary Quarterly,* 3d ser., 1:65–82.   (21)

[68]   Curry, Richard O. 1963. "Lord Dunmore—Tool of Land Jobbers?" *West Virginia History* 24:289–95.   (37)

[69]   Davis, T. Frederick, comp. 1935. "History of Juan Ponce de León's Voyages to Florida: Source Records." *Florida Historical Quarterly* 14:1–70.   (3)

[70]   Deagan, Kathleen A. 1973. "Mestizaje in Colonial San Augustine." *Ethnohistory* 20:55–65.   (44)

[71]   ———. 1978. "Cultures in Transition: Fusion and Assimilation among the Eastern Timucua." In *Tacachale*, ed. J. T. Milanich and S. Proctor, pp. 89–119. See [200].   (11)

*[72]   Debo, Angie. 1934. *The Rise and Fall of the Choctaw Republic*. Norman: University of Oklahoma Press.   (55)

[73]   De Braham, William G. 1971. *Report of the General Survey in the Southern District of North America*. Edited by Louis De Vorsey. Columbia: University of South Carolina Press.   (36)

[74]   Del Papa, Eugene M. 1975. "The Royal Proclamation of 1763: Its Effects upon Virginia Land Companies." *Virginia Magazine of History and Biography* 83:406–11.   (38)

[75]   DeRosier, Arthur H. 1960. "Negotiations for the Removal of the Choctaws:
United States Policies of 1820 and
1830." *Chronicles of Oklahoma* 38:85–
100.   (51)

[76]   ———. 1967. "Andrew Jackson and
Negotiations for the Removal of the
Choctaw Indians." *Historian* 29:343–62.   (51)

[77]   ———. 1970. *The Removal of the Choctaw
Indians.* Knoxville: University of Tennessee Press.   (51)

[78]   De Vorsey, Louis, Jr. 1961. "The
Virginia-Cherokee Boundary of 1771."
*East Tennessee Historical Society Publica-
tions* 33:17–31.   (37)

[79]   ———. 1966. *The Indian Boundary in the
Southern Colonies, 1763–1775.* Chapel
Hill: University of North Carolina
Press.   (36)

[80]   ———. 1970. "Indian Boundaries in
Colonial Georgia." *Georgia Historical
Quarterly* 54:63–78.   (37)

[81]   Din, Gilbert C. 1969. "Immigration Policy of Esteban Miro." *Southwestern Historical Quarterly* 73:155–75.   (44)

[82] ———. 1975. "Spain's Immigration Policy and Efforts in Louisiana during the American Revolution." *Louisiana Studies* 14:241–57. (44)

[83] ———. 1978. "Protecting the 'Barrera': Spain's Defenses in Louisiana, 1763–1779." *Louisiana History* 19:183–211. (43)

[84] Dobyns, Henry F. 1966. "Estimating Aboriginal American Population: An Appraisal of Techniques with a New Hemispheric Estimate." *Current Anthropology* 7:395–416 and "Reply," 7:440–44. (xi)

[85] ———. 1976. *Native American Historical Demography: A Critical Bibliography.* Bloomington: Indiana University Press for Newberry Library. (x)

[86] Downes, Randolph C. 1934. "Dunmore's War: An Interpretation." *Mississippi Valley Historical Review* 21:311–30. (37)

[87] ———. 1936. "Cherokee-American Relations in the Upper Tennessee Valley, 1776–1791." *East Tennessee Historical Society Publications* 8:35–53. (48)

[88]   ———. 1942. "Creek-American Relations, 1790–1795." *Journal of Southern History* 8:350–73.   (48)

[89]   Dunn, William Edward. 1917. *Spanish and French Rivalry in the Gulf Region of the United States, 1678–1702.* Austin: University of Texas Press.   (18)

[90]   Earle, Carville V. 1977. "The First English Towns of North America." *Georgia Review,* January, pp. 34–50.   (22)

[91]   Eccles, W. J. 1972. *France in America.* New York: Harper and Row.   (32)

[92]   Fairbanks, Charles. 1978. "The Ethno-Archaeology of the Florida Seminoles." In *Tacachale,* ed. J. T. Milanich and S. Proctor, pp. 163–93. See [200].   (56)

[93]   Fausz, J. Frederick. 1977. "The Powhatan Uprising of 1622: A Historical Study of Ethnocentrism and Cultural Conflict." Ph.D. diss., College of William and Mary. Ann Arbor: University Microfilms.   (24)

[94]   ———. 1979. "George Thorpe, New-
       mattanew (Powhatan War Chief), and
       the Powhatan Uprising of 1622." *Vir-
       ginia Cavalcade,* winter, pp. 111–17.   (24)

[95]   Ferguson, Clyde R. 1971. "Andrew
       Pickens and United States Policy
       toward the Creek Nation." *Kansas Quar-
       terly* 3:21–28.   (46)

[96]   ———. 1979. "Confrontation at Col-
       eraine (1796): Creeks, Georgians and
       Federalist Indian Policy." *Southern His-
       tory Quarterly,* spring, pp. 224–43.   (46)

[97]   Fogelson, Raymond D. 1978. *The
       Cherokees: A Critical Bibliography*.
       Bloomington: Indiana University Press
       for Newberry Library.   (1, 56)

[98]   Folmer, Henry. 1953. *Franco-Spanish
       Rivalry in North America, 1524–1763*.
       Glendale, Calif.: Arthur H. Clark.   (18)

[99]   Forbes, Jack D. 1968. "Frontiers in
       American History and the Role of the
       Frontier Historian." *Ethnohistory*
       15:203–5.   (x)

*[100]   Foreman, Grant. 1932. *Indian Removal: The Emigration of the Five Civilized Tribes of Indians.* Norman: University of Oklahoma Press. Reprinted, 1976.   (51)

*[101]   ———. 1934. *The Five Civilized Tribes: Cherokee, Chickasaw, Choctaw, Creek, Seminole.* Norman: University of Oklahoma Press, 1974.   (55)

[102]   Formisano, Ronald P. 1976. "Toward a Reorientation of Jacksonian Politics: A Review of the Literature, 1959–1975." *Journal of American History* 63:42–65.   (53)

[103]   Franklin, W. Neil. 1932. "Virginia and the Cherokee Indian Trade, 1673–1752." *East Tennessee Historical Society Publications* 4:3–21.   (29)

[104]   ———. 1933. "Virginia and the Cherokee Indian Trade, 1753–1775." *East Tennessee Historical Society Publications* 5:22–38.   (29)

[105]   French, Benjamin Franklin, ed. 1846–53. *Historical Collections of Louisiana, Embracing Many Rare and Valuable Documents Relating to the Natural, Civil and Political History of That State.* 3 vols. New York: Wiley and Putman.   (7)

[106]   Ganyard, Robert L. 1968. "Threat from
        the West: North Carolina and the
        Cherokee, 1776–1778." *North Carolina
        Historical Review* 45:47–66.   (41)

[107]   García, Genaro, ed. 1902. *Dos Antiguas
        Relaciónes de la Florida, Publicalas por
        Primera Vez.* Mexico: Tip. y Lit. de J.
        Aguilar Vera y Comp.   (11)

[108]   Gearing, Fred. 1962. *Priests and War-
        riors: Social Structures for Cherokee Politics
        in the 18th Century.* Memoir 93. Wash-
        ington, D.C.: American Anthropologi-
        cal Association.   (48)

[109]   Geiger, Maynard J. 1937. *The Francis-
        can Conquest of Florida (1573–1618).*
        Washington, D.C.: Catholic University
        of America Press.   (14)

[110]   Gibson, Arrell M. 1971. *The Chickasaws.*
        Norman: University of Oklahoma
        Press.   (54)

[111]   Gibson, Charles. 1978. "Conquest,
        Capitulation, and Indian Treaties."
        American Historical Review 83:1–15.   (31)

[112]   Giraud, Marcel. 1953–. *Histoire de la
        Louisiane française.* Paris: University of

France Press. New ed., vol. 1, *A History of Louisiana: The Reign of Louis XIV, 1698–1715*, trans. Joseph C. Lambert, Baton Rouge: Louisiana State University Press, 1974.   (32)

[113] Goff, John H. "The Path to Oakfuskee: Upper Trading Route in Alabama to the Creek Indians." *Georgia Historical Quarterly* 39:1–35, 152–71.   (35)

[114] Gold, Robert L. 1965. "The Settlement of the Pensacola Indians in New Spain, 1763–1770." *Hispanic American Historical Review* 45:567–76.   (44)

[115] Goodstein, Anita A. 1976. "Leadership on the Nashville Frontier." *Tennessee Historical Quarterly* 35:175–98.   (42)

[116] Goodwin, Gary C. 1977. *Cherokees in Transition: A Study of Changing Culture and Environment prior to 1775*. Chicago: University of Chicago Department of Geography.   (49)

[117] Green, Michael D. 1973. "Federal-State Conflict in the Administration of Indian Policy: Georgia, Alabama, and the Creeks, 1824–1834." Ph.D. diss., University of Iowa.   (52)

[118]   ———. 1980. "Alexander McGillivray."
In *Perspectives on American Indian Leader-ship*, ed. R. David Edmunds, pp. 41–63.
Lincoln: University of Nebraska Press.   (41)

[119]   ———. 1980. *The Creeks: A Critical Bib-liography.* Bloomington: Indiana Uni-versity Press for Newberry Library.   (1, 55)

[120]   Grinde, Donald, Jr. 1977. "Native
American Slavery in the Southern Col-onies." *Indian Historian* 10:38–42.   (28)

[121]   Hakluyt, Richard, trans. 1609. *Virginia
Richly Valued, by the Description of the
Mainland of Florida, Her Next Neighbour;
out of the Four Yeeres Continuall Trauell
and Discouerie . . . of Don Fernando de
Soto. . . . Written by a Portugall Gentleman
of Eluas.* London: K. Kyngston for M.
Lownes. Reprinted in [105].   (6)

[122]   Halbert, H. S., and T. H. Ball. 1895.
The Creek War of 1813 and 1814.
Chicago: Donohue and Henneberry.
Reprinted, with introduction by Frank
L. Owsley, Jr., Birmingham: University
of Alabama Press, 1969.   (55)

[123]   Halliburton, Richard, Jr. 1976. *Red over
Black: Black Slavery among the Cherokee*

Indians. Westport, Conn.: Greenwood
Press.   (26, 49)

*[124]   ———. 1977. "Red over Black: Black
Slavery among the Cherokees." *American History Illustrated* 11:12–19.   (26)

[125]   Hamer, Philip M. 1925. "Anglo-French
Rivalry in the Cherokee Country,
1754–57." *North Carolina Historical Review* 2:303–22.   (34)

[126]   ———. 1931. "The Wataugans and the
Cherokee Indians in 1776." *East Tennessee Historical Society Publications* 3:108–
26.   (34)

[127]   Hamilton, Peter J. 1910. *Colonial
Mobile*. Rev. and enl. ed., Mobile, Ala.:
First National Bank of Mobile, 1952.
Reprint of 1910 edition, ed. Charles G.
Summersell, Birmingham: University
of Alabama Press, 1976.   (32)

[128]   Hassig, Ross. 1974. "Internal Conflict
in the Creek War of 1813–1814."
Ethnohistory 21:251–71.   (55)

[129]   Herbert, John. 1936. *Journal of Colonel
John Herbert*. Edited by A. S. Salley. Co-

lumbia: South Carolina Historical
Commission.   (35)

[130]   Hernández, José B. 1976. "Opposing
        Views of La Florida: Álvar Núñez
        Cabeza de Vaca and El Inca Garcilaso
        del la Vega." *Florida Historical Quarterly*
        55:170–80.   (7)

[131]   Herrera y Tordesillas, Antonio de.
        1601–15. *Historia general de los hechos de
        los castellaños en las islas i tierra firme del
        mar oceano.* 4 vols. Madrid: Imprenta
        Real. Reissued, ed. Andrés González de
        Barcia Caraballido y Zuñiga, 9 vols.
        Imprenta Real, 1726–27. Reprinted, 17
        vols., Madrid: Tipografía de Archivos,
        1934–57.   (4)

[132]   Higginbotham, Jay. 1978. "Henri de
        Tonti's Mission to the Chickasaw, 1702."
        Louisiana History 19:285–96.   (31)

[133]   Hodge, Frederick Webb, ed. 1907.
        "The Narrative of Álvar Núñez Cabeza
        de Vaca." In *Spanish Explorers in the
        Southern United States, 1528–1543*, ed.
        F. W. Hodge and Theodore H. Lewis,
        pp. 1–126. New York: Charles
        Scribner's Sons, 1907 (translation of the

first edition of 1542 published at Zamora, Spain).   (5)

[134]   Holmes, Jack D. L. 1965. *Gayoso: Spanish Governor in the Mississippi Valley, 1789–1799*. Baton Rouge: Louisiana State University Press.   (43)

[135]   ———. 1968. "The Choctaws in 1795." *Alabama Historical Quarterly* 30:33–49.   (55)

[136]   ———. 1969. "Spanish Treaties with the West Florida Indians, 1784–1802." *Florida Historical Quarterly* 48:140–54.   (43)

[137]   ———. 1975. "The Role of Blacks in Spanish Alabama: The Mobile District, 1780–1813." *Alabama Historical Quarterly* 37:5–18.   (26)

[138]   ———. 1975. "Spanish Policy toward the Southern Indians in the 1790's." In *Four Centuries of Southern Indians*, ed. Charles Hudson, pp. 65–82. Athens: University of Georgia Press.   (43)

[139]   ———. 1978. "Up the Tombigbee with Spaniards: Juan de la Villebeuvre and the Treaty of Boucfouca (1793)." *Alabama Historical Quarterly* 40:51–61.   (43)

[140] Honour, Hugh. 1975. *The New Golden Land: European Images of America from the Discoveries to the Present Time*. New York: Pantheon Books.   (20)

[141] Horsman, Reginald. 1968. "American Indian Policy and the Origins of Manifest Destiny." *University of Birmingham Historical Journal* 11:12–40.   (52)

[142] Hryneiwici, Richard J. 1964. "The Creek Treaty of Washington, 1826." *Georgia Historical Quarterly* 48:425–41.   (52)

[143] ———. 1968. "The Creek Treaty of November 15, 1827." *Georgia Historical Quarterly* 52:1–15.   (52)

[144] Huddleston, Lee E. 1967. *Origins of the American Indians: European Concepts, 1492–1729*. Austin: University of Texas Press.   (20)

*[145] Hudson, Charles. 1976. *The Southeastern Indians*. Knoxville: University of Tennessee Press.   (1, 55)

[146] Hulton, Paul, and David B. Quinn. 1964. *The American Drawings of John White, 1577–1590*. 2 vols. London: Trustees of the British Museum.   (19)

*[147] Ivers, Larry. 1974. *British Drums on the Southern Frontier.* Chapel Hill: University of North Carolina Press.   (39)

[148] Jennings, Francis. 1975. *The Invasion of America: Indians, Colonialism, and the Cant of Conquest.* Chapel Hill: University of North Carolina Press.   (x)

[149] Johnson, Cecil. 1943. *British West Florida, 1763–1783.* New Haven: Yale University Press. Reprinted, Hamden, Conn.: Archon Books, 1971.   (43)

[150] Johnson, J. G. 1923. "The Yamassee Revolt of 1597 and the Destruction of the Georgia Missions." *Georgia Historical Quarterly* 7:44–53.   (16)

[151] Johnston, James H. 1929. "Documentary Evidence of Relations of Negroes and Indians." *Journal of Negro History* 14:21–43.   (25)

[152] Jones, Howard M. 1964. *O Strange New World: American Culture; the Formative Years.* New York: Viking Press.   (20)

[153] Jones, Hugh. 1724. *The Present State of Virginia.* London: J. Clarke. Reprinted, New York: J. Sabin, 1865.   (29)

[154] Jones, Jerome W. 1961. "The Established Virginia Church and the Conversion of Negroes and Indians, 1620–1760." *Journal of Negro History* 46:12–23.   (25)

[155] Kawashima, Yasuhide. 1978. "The Native Americans and White Man's Law before 1800." *Indian Historian* 11:22–27.   (24)

[156] Keith, Alice B., ed. 1952. *The John Gray Blount Papers.* Raleigh, N.C.: State Department of Archives.   (47)

[157] Kellogg, Louise Phelps. 1931. "France and the Mississippi Valley." *Mississippi Valley Historical Review* 18:3–22.   (32)

[158] ———, ed. 1917. *Early Narratives of the Northwest, 1634–1699.* New York: Barnes and Noble.   (31)

[159] Kidwell, Clara Sue, and Charles Roberts. 1980. *The Choctaws: A Critical Bibliography.* Bloomington: Indiana University Press for Newberry Library.   (1)

[160] Kimmel, Ross M. 1976. "Free Blacks in Seventeenth Century Maryland." *Maryland Historical Magazine* 11:19–25.   (25)

[161]   Kinnaird, Lawrence, ed. 1945. *Spain in the Mississippi Valley, 1765–1794*. Annual Report of the American Historical Association.   (18)

[162]   Knight, Oliver. 1954. "Cherokee Society under the Stress of Removal, 1820–1846." *Chronicles of Oklahoma* 32:414–28.   (51)

[163]   La Harpe, Bernard de. 1831. *Journal historique de l'establissement des français à la Louisiane*. Paris: Hector Lossange.   (32)

[164]   Lanning, John T. 1935. *The Spanish Missions of Georgia*. Chapel Hill: University of North Carolina Press.   (15)

[165]   ———. 1936. *The Diplomatic History of Georgia*. Chapel Hill: University of North Carolina Press.   (17)

[166]   Larson, Lewis H. 1978. "Historic Guale Indians of the Georgia Coast and the Impact of the Spanish Mission Effort." In *Tacachale*, ed. J. T. Milanich and S. Proctor, pp. 120–49. See [200].   (16)

[167]   Lauber, Almon W. 1913. *Indian Slavery in Colonial Times within the Present Limits*

of the United States. New York: Columbia
University Press.   (29)

[168]   Laudonnière, René Goulaine de. 1975
        [1586]. *Three Voyages.* Translated with
        an introduction and notes by Charles E.
        Bennett. Gainesville: University Presses
        of Florida. Originally published in
        French as *L'histoire notable de la Floride,
        située en Indes Occidentales, contenant les
        trois voyages faits en icelle par certains
        capitaines et pilotes français.* . . . Paris: G.
        Auray, 1586.   (10)

*[169] Lee, E. Lawrence. 1963. *Indian Wars in
        North Carolina, 1663–1763.* Raleigh:
        North Carolina Department of Ar-
        chives and History.   (34)

[170]   Leonard, Irving A., ed. 1939. *Spanish
        Approaches to Pensacola, 1689–1693.*
        Translated with notes by I. A. Leonard,
        foreword by James A. Robertson. Al-
        buquerque: Quivira Society.   (18)

[171]   LePage du Pratz, Antoine Simon. 1758.
        *Histoire de la Louisiane contenant la dé-
        couverte de ce vaste pays; sa geographique;
        un voyage dans les terres; l'histoire na-
        turelle, les moeurs, coutumes et religion des*

*naturels, avec leurs origines; deux voyages
dans le nord du nouveau Méxique, dont un
jusqu'à la Mer du Sud.* 3 vols. Paris: De
Burre. 1st English ed. published as *The
History of Louisiana, or of the Western
Parts of Virginia and Carolina.* . . . London: T. Becket and P. A. De Hondt,
1763. Reprinted, 1774. Facsimile of
1774 English ed., ed. Joseph G. Tregle,
Jr., Baton Rouge: Louisiana State University Press, 1975.   (32)

[172] Lewis, Clifford M., and Albert J.
Loomie, eds. 1953. *The Spanish Jesuit
Mission in Virginia, 1570–1572.* Chapel
Hill: University of North Carolina
Press.   (14)

[173] Lewis, Theodore H., ed. 1907. "The
Narrative of the Expedition of Her-
nando de Soto by the Gentleman of El-
vas." *Spanish Explorers in the Southern
United States, 1528–1543,* ed. F. W.
Hodge and T. H. Lewis, pp. 127–272.
Original Narratives of Early American
History, gen. ed. J. Franklin Jameson.
New York: Charles Scribner's Sons
(Reprint of the 1866 translation by
Buckingham Smith, found in Bourne
[29].)   (6)

[174]   Littlefield, Daniel. 1979. *Africans and Creeks: From the Colonial Period to the Civil War*. Westport, Conn.: Greenwood Press.   (26, 49)

[175]   Litton, Gaston. 1941. "The Journal of a Party of Emigrating Creek Indians, 1835–1836." *Journal of Southern History* 7:225–42.   (52)

[176]   Lorant, Stefan, ed. 1946. *The New World: Notes on the French Settlements in Florida, 1562–1565*. New York: Duell, Sloan, and Pearce.   (10, 19)

[177]   Lowery, Woodbury. 1901, 1905. *The Spanish Settlements within the Present Limits of the United States, 1513–1574*. 2 vols. vol. 1, *1513–1561;* vol. 2, *Florida, 1562–1574*. New York: G. P. Putnam's Sons. Reprinted, New York: Russell and Russell, 1959.   (3)

[178]   Lurie, Nancy O. 1959. "Indian Cultural Adjustment to European Civilization." In *Seventeenth-Century America: Essays in Colonial History*, ed. James M. Smith, pp. 33–60. Chapel Hill: University of North Carolina Press.   (22)

[179]   Lyon, Eugene. 1976. *The Enterprise of Florida: Pedro Menéndez de Avilés and the Spanish Conquest, 1565–1568*. Gainesville: University Presses of Florida.   (12)

[180]   McDaniel, Mary Jane. 1971. "Relations between the Creek Indians, Georgia, and the United States, 1783–1797." Ph.D. diss., Mississippi State University.   (46)

[181]   McDermott, John F. 1965. *The French in the Mississippi Valley*. Urbana: University of Illinois Press.   (32)

[182]   McDowell, William L., Jr. 1955. *The Colonial Records of South Carolina: Documents Relating to Indian Affairs, 1754–1765*. Columbia: South Carolina Department of Archives and History.   (40)

[183]   McKee, Jesse O., and John A. Schlenker. 1980. *The Choctaws: Cultural Evolution of a Native American Tribe*. Jackson: University Press of Mississippi.   (55)

[184]   McLaughlin, William G., and Walter H. Conser, Jr. 1977. "The Cherokees in Transition. A Statistical Analysis of the Federal Cherokee Census of 1835." *Journal of American History* 64:687–701.   (51)

*[185]   McReynolds, Edwin C. 1957. *The Seminoles.* Norman: University of Oklahoma Press.   (56)

[186]   McWilliams, R. G. 1967. "Iberville and the Southern Indians." *Alabama Review* 22:243–62.   (32)

[187]   Magnaghi, Russell M. 1975. "The Role of Indian Slavery in Colonial St. Louis." *Bulletin of the Missouri Historical Society* 31:264–72.   (28)

[188]   Malone, Henry T. 1956. *Cherokees of the Old South: A People in Transition.* Athens: University of Georgia Press.   (57)

[189]   Marrant, John. 1788 [1785]. *A Narrative of the Lord's Wonderful Dealings with John Marrant, a Black (Now Gone to Preach the Gospel in Nova Scotia), Born in New York, in North America, Taken Down from His Own Relation, Arranged, Corrected, and Published, by the Rev. Mr. Aldridge.* 6th ed., with additions and notes. London: Gilbert and Plummer. Reprinted, in *Held Captive by Indians: Selected Captivity Narratives, 1642–1836,* Knoxville: University of Tennessee Press, 1973. See [302].   (35)

[190] Masterson, William H. 1954. *William Blount*. Baton Rouge: Louisiana State University Press.   (47)

[191] Matter, Robert A. 1975. "Missions in the Defense of Spanish Florida, 1566– 1710." *Florida Historical Quarterly* 54:18–38.   (15)

[192] Meinig, D. W. 1972. "American Wests: Preface to a Geographical Interpretation." *Annals of the Association of American Geographers* 62:159–84.   (36)

[193] ———. 1978. "The Continuous Shaping of America: A Prospectus for Geographers and Historians." *American Historical Review* 83:1186–1205.   (36)

[194] Menéndez de Avilés, Pedro. 1894 [1565–66]. "Seven Letters written to the King by the General Pedro Menéndez de Avilés. . . ." Translated by Henry Ware. *Proceedings of the Massachusetts Historical Society*, 2d ser., 8(1892– 94):416–68. Also see [279].   (12)

[195] Meriwether, Robert I. 1941. *The Expansion of South Carolina, 1729–1765*. Kingsport, Tenn.: Kingsport Press.   (40)

[196]   Merrell, James H. 1979. "Cultural
        Continuity among the Piscataway Indi-
        ans of Colonial Maryland." *William and
        Mary Quarterly*, 3d ser., 36:548–70.   (37)

[197]   Merrens, H. Roy. 1964. *Colonial North
        Carolina in the 18th Century: A Study in
        Historical Geography*. Chapel Hill: Uni-
        versity of North Carolina Press.   (36)

[198]   ———. 1965. "Historical Geography
        and Early American History." *William
        and Mary Quarterly*, 3d ser., 22:529–48.   (36)

[199]   Milanich, Jerald T. 1978. "The Western
        Timucua: Patterns of Acculturation
        and Change." In *Tacachale*, ed. J. T.
        Milanich and S. Proctor, pp. 59–88.
        See [200].   (11)

[200]   Milanich, Jerald T., and Samuel Proc-
        tor, eds. 1978. *Tacachale: Essays on the
        Indians of Florida and Southeastern Geor-
        gia during the Historic Period*. Gainesville:
        University Presses of Florida.   (10)

[201]   Milanich, Jerald T., and William C.
        Sturtevant, eds. 1972. *Francisco Pareja's
        1613 Confessionario: A Documentary
        Source for Timucuan Ethnography*. Tal-

lahassee: Florida Department of State, Division of Archives, History, and Records Management.   (16)

[202]   Milfort, Louis LeClerc de. 1802. *Memoire ou coup-d'oeil rapide sur mes différens voyages et mon séjour dans la nation Crëck.* Paris: De l'Impr. de Giguet et Michaud. New ed., trans. Geraldine De Courcy, ed. John Francis McDermott, *Memoirs; or, A Cursory Glance at My Different Travels and My Sojourn in the Creek Nation*, Chicago: Lakeside Press, 1956. Reprinted, Savannah, Ga.: Beehive Press, 1972.   (47)

*[203]   Milling, Chapman J. 1940. *Red Carolinians.* Chapel Hill: University of North Carolina Press. Reprinted, Columbia: University of South Carolina Press, 1969.   (40)

[204]   Mooney, James. 1900. "Myths of the Cherokees." In *Nineteenth Annual Report of the Bureau of American Ethnology*, part 1, pp. 3–576. Washington, D.C.: Government Printing Office. Reprinted, New York: Johnson, 1970.   (57)

[205]   Morgan, Edmund S. 1971. "The First American Boom: Virginia, 1618–1630." *William and Mary Quarterly*, 3d ser., 28:169–98.   (23)

[206]   ———. 1971. "The Labor Problem at Jamestown." *American Historical Review* 76:595–611.   (23)

[207]   ———. 1975. *American Slavery, American Freedom: The Ordeal of Colonial Virginia.* New York: W. W. Norton.   (23)

[208]   Moulton, Gary E. 1978. *John Ross: Cherokee Chief.* Athens: University of Georgia Press.   (50, 51)

[209]   Mowat, Charles L. 1943. *East Florida as a British Province, 1763–1784.* Berkeley: University of California Press.   (40)

[210]   Murdoch, Richard K. 1951. *The Georgia-Florida Frontier, 1793–1976: Spanish Reaction to French Intrigue and American Designs.* Berkeley: University of California Press.   (47)

[211]   Nash, Gary B. 1972. "The Image of the Indian in the Southern Colonial Mind."

William and Mary Quarterly, 3d ser.,
29:197–230.   (20)

*[212]   ———. 1974. *Red, White and Black: The
Peoples of Early America*. Englewood,
N.J.: Prentice-Hall.   (xv)

[213]   Neasham, V. Aubrey. 1939. "Spain's
Emigrants to the New World, 1492–
1592." *Hispanic American Historical Re-
view* 19:147–60.   (15)

[214]   Núñez Cabeza de Vaca, Álvar. 1905
[1542]. *The Journey of Álvar Núñez
Cabeza de Vaca and His Companions from
Florida to the Pacific, 1528–1536, Trans-
lated from His Own Narrative by Fanny
Bandelier, Together with the Report of
Father Marcos of Nizza, and a Letter from
the Viceroy Mendoza*. Edited and with an
introduction by Adolph F. Bandelier.
New York: A. S. Barnes.   (5)

[215]   O'Donnell, James H., III. 1965. "Alexander McGillivray: Training for
Leadership, 1777–1783." *Georgia His-
torical Quarterly* 49:172–86.   (41, 45)

[216]   ———. 1973. *The Southern Indians in the
American Revolution*. Knoxville: Univer-
sity of Tennessee Press.   (41)

*[217]   ———. 1975. *The Georgia Indian Frontier, 1773-1783.* Atlanta: Georgia Commission for the National Bicentennial Celebration and the Georgia Department of Education.   (41)

[218]   ———. 1976. *The Cherokees of North Carolina in the American Revolution.* Raleigh, N.C.: Department of Cultural Resources, Division of Archives and History.   (41)

[219]   Olson, Gary D. 1967-68. "Loyalists and the American Revolution: Thomas Brown and the South Carolina Backcountry, 1775-1776." *South Carolina Historical Magazine* 68:201-19; 69:44-56.   (42)

[220]   ———. 1970. Thomas Brown, Loyalist Partisan, and the Revolutionary War in Georgia, 1778-1782." *Georgia Historical Quarterly* 54:1-19, 183-208.   (42)

[221]   Oré, Luís Gerónimo de. 1936 [?1617-1620]. *The Martyrs of Florida, 1513-1616.* Translated, with biographical introduction and notes, by Maynard Geiger. Franciscan Studies 18. New York: Joseph F. Wagner.   (16)

[222]   Oviedo y Valdés, Gonzálo Fernández
de. 1851–55 [1535–?]. *La historia general y natural de las Indias, Islas y
Tierra-Firme del Mar Oceano.* 4 vols. Madrid: Imprenta de la Real Academia de
la Historia.   (4)

[223]   Parkman, Francis. 1865. *Pioneers of
France in the New World.* Boston: Little,
Brown. Rev. ed., Toronto: G. N.
Morang, 1901. Reprinted, New York:
AMS, 1969.   (12)

[224]   Pearce, Roy Harvey. 1953. *The Savages
of America: A Study of the Indian and the
Idea of Civilization.* Baltimore: Johns
Hopkins Press. Revised ed., Baltimore:
Johns Hopkins Press, 1965.   (21)

[225]   Pearson, Fred L., Jr. 1975. "The
Arguelles Inspection of Guale: Decem-
ber 21, 1677–January 10, 1678." *Geor-
gia Historical Quarterly* 59:210–22.   (17)

[226]   Peckham, Howard, and Charles Gibson, eds. 1969. *Attitudes of Colonial Powers toward the American Indian.* Salt Lake
City: University of Utah Press.   (31)

[227]   Pennington, Edgar Legare. 1935. "The
Reverend Francis le Jau's Work among

Indians and Negro Slaves." *Journal of Southern History* 1:1–17. (26)

[228] Perdue, Theda. 1977. "Rising from the Ashes: The Cherokee Phoenix as an Ethnohistorical Source." *Ethnohistory* 24:207–18. (57)

[229] ———. 1979. *Slavery and the Evolution of Cherokee Society, 1540–1866.* Knoxville: University of Tennessee Press. (26, 27, 49)

[230] Phillips, Philip, James A. Ford, and James B. Griffin. 1951. "Archaeological Survey in the Lower Mississippi Alluvial Valley, 1940–47." Papers of the Peabody Museum 25. Cambridge: Peabody Museum. Reprinted, Millwood, N.Y.: Kraus Reprint, 1974. (8)

[231] Porter, Frank W., III. 1979. "A Century of Accommodation: The Maryland Nanticoke Indians in Colonial Maryland." *Maryland Historical Magazine,* June, pp. 175–92. (37)

[232] Porter, Kenneth W. 1932. "Relations between Negroes and Indians within the Present Limits of the United States." *Journal of Negro History* 17:287–367. Reprinted in [238]. (25)

[233]   ———. 1933. "Notes Supplementary to 'Relations between Negroes and Indians.'" *Journal of Negro History* 18:282–321. Reprinted in [238].   (25)

[234]   ———. 1943. "Florida Slaves and Free Negroes in the Seminole War." *Journal of Negro History* 28:390–421.   (56)

[235]   ———. 1945. "Negroes and the East Florida Annexation Plot, 1811–1813." *Journal of Negro History* 30:9–29.   (56)

[236]   ———. 1948. "Negroes on the Southern Frontier, 1670–1763." *Journal of Negro History* 33:53–78.   (25)

[237]   ———. 1951. "Negroes and the Seminole War." *Journal of Negro History* 36:249–80.   (56)

[238]   ———. 1971. *The Negro on the American Frontier.* New York: Arno Press.   (25)

[239]   Pound, Merritt B. 1951. *Benjamin Hawkins: Indian Agent.* Athens: University of Georgia Press.   (46)

[240]   Priestly, Herbert Ingram. 1936. *Tristan de Luna, Conquistador of the Old South: A*

Study of Spanish Imperial Policy. Glendale, Calif.: Arthur H. Clark.   (9)

[241] ———, ed. 1928. *The Luna Papers: Documents relating to the Expedition of Don Tristan de Luna y Arellano for the Conquest of La Florida in 1559–1561.* 2 vols. Publications of the Florida State Historical Society 8. Deland: Florida State Historical Society. Reprinted, Freeport, N.Y.: Books for Libraries Press, 1971.   (9)

[242] Prucha, Francis Paul. 1969. "Andrew Jackson's Indian Policy: A Reassessment." *Journal of American History* 56:527–39.   (53)

[243] Purdy, Barbara A. 1977. "Weapons, Strategies, and Tactics of the Europeans and the Indians in 16th and 17th Century Florida." *Florida Historical Quarterly* 56:259–76.   (17)

*[244] Quattlebaum, Paul. 1956. *The Land Called Chicora: The Carolinas under Spanish Rule with French Intrusions, 1520–1670.* Gainesville: University of Florida Press. Reprinted, Spartanburg, S.C.: Reprint Company, 1973.   (9)

[245]   Quinn, David Beers. 1974. *England and the Discovery of America, 1481–1620: From the Bristol Voyages of the Fifteenth Century to the Pilgrim Settlement in Plymouth.* New York: Knopf.   (19)

[246]   ———. 1977. *North America from Earliest Discovery to First Settlements: The Norse Voyages to 1612.* New York: Harper and Row.   (2, 9)

[247]   ———, ed. 1955. *The Roanoke Voyages, 1584–1590: Documents to Illustrate the English Voyages to North America under the Patent Granted to Sir Walter Raleigh in 1584.* London: Hakluyt Society. Reprinted, Millwood, N.Y.: Kraus Reprint.   (18)

[248]   ———, ed. 1979. *New American World: A Documentary History of North America to 1612.* 5 vols. New York: Arno Press and Hector Bye.   (3, 4, 9)

[249]   Quitt, Martin H. 1976. "Jackson, Indians, and Psychohistory: A Review Essay." *History of Childhood Quarterly* 3:543–51.   (53)

[250]   Ramsay, Robert W. 1965. *Carolina Cradle*. Chapel Hill: University of North Carolina Press.   (40)

[251]   Reese, Trevor R. 1958. "Georgia in Anglo-Spanish Diplomacy, 1736–1739." *William and Mary Quarterly*, 3d ser., 15:168–90.   (39)

[252]   ———. 1959. "Britain's Military Support of Georgia in the War of 1739–1748." *Georgia Historical Quarterly* 43:1–10.   (39)

[253]   Reid, John P. 1970. *A Law of Blood: The Primitive Law of the Cherokee People*. New York: New York University Press.   (48)

[254]   ———. 1976. *A Better Kind of Hatchet: Law, Trade, and Diplomacy in the Cherokee Nation during the Early Years of European Contact*. University Park, Pa.: Penn State Press.   (48)

[255]   Ribaut, Jean. 1927 [1563]. *The Whole and True Discouerye of Terra Florida: A Facsimile Reprint of the London Edition of 1563, Together with a Transcript of an English Version in the British Museum with Notes by H. M. Biggar, and a Biography by*

Jeannette Thurber Connor. Publications of the Florida State Historical Society 7. Deland: Florida State Historical Society.   (10)

[256] Robert, V. Haynes. 1977. "Life on the Mississippi Frontier, 1776–1780: Case of Matthew Phelps." *Journal of Mississippi History,* February, pp. 1–15.   (47)

[257] Robertson, James Alexander, trans, and ed. 1932–33. *True Relation of the Hardships Suffered by Governor Fernando de Soto and Certain Portuguese Gentlemen during the Discovery of the Province of Florida: Now Newly Set Forth by a Gentleman of Elvas.* Vol. 1. Facsimile reproduction of 1557 Portuguese edition entitled *Relacam Verdadeira.* . . . Vol. 2. English translation with notes. Deland: Florida State Historical Society.   (6)

[258] Robinson, W. Stitt, Jr. 1952. "Indian Education and Missions in Colonial Virginia." *Journal of Southern History* 18:152–68.   (30)

*[259] ———. 1979. *The Southern Colonial Frontier, 1607–1763.* Albuquerque: University of New Mexico Press.   (30)

[260]   Rogin, Michael P. 1975. *Fathers and Children: Andrew Jackson and the Subjugation of the American Indian.* New York: Alfred Knopf.   (53)

[261]   Ross, Mary. 1923. "French Intrusions and Indian Uprisings in Georgia and South Carolina, 1577–1580." *Georgia Historical Quarterly* 7:251–81.   (19)

[262]   ———. 1924. "The French on the Savannah, 1605." *Georgia Historical Quarterly* 8:167–94.   (32)

[263]   ———. 1926. "The Restoration of the Spanish Missions in Georgia, 1598–1606." *Georgia Historical Quarterly* 10:171–99.   (16)

[264]   Rothrock, Mary. 1929. "Carolina Traders among the Overhill Cherokees, 1690–1760." *East Tennessee Historical Society Publications* 1:3–18.   (34)

[265]   Rowland, Dunbar, and A. G. Sanders. 1927–32. *Mississippi Provincial Archives: The French Dominion, 1704–1743.* 3 vols. Press of the Mississippi Department of Archives and History.   (32)

[266]   Royce, Charles C. 1975. *The Cherokee Nation of Indians.* Chicago: Aldine.   (57)

[267]   Ruidiáz y Caravia, Eugenio, ed. 1893. *La Florida: Su conquista y colonización por Pedro Menéndez de Avilés.* 2 vols. Madrid: Real Academia de la Historia.   (11)

[268]   Satz, Ronald N. 1975. *American Indian Policy in the Jacksonian Era.* Lincoln: University of Nebraska Press.   (53)

*[269]   Sauer, Carl Ortwin. 1971. *Sixteenth Century North America: The Land and the People as Seen by the First Europeans.* Berkeley: University of California Press.   (2)

[270]   Schlenker, Jon A. 1975. "An Historical Analysis of the Family Life of the Choctaw Indians." *Southern Quarterly* 13:323–34.   (55)

[271]   Serrano y Sanz, Manuel. 1916. *España y los Indios Cherokis y Chactas en la segunda mital del siglo XVIII.* Sevilla: Tip. de la Guia oficial.   (43)

[272]   ———, ed. 1906. *Relación de los naufragios comentarios de Álvar Núñez Cabeza de Vaca . . . illustrados con varios docu-*

mentos inéditos. 2 vols. Madrid: V. Suárez. (Reprint of 1555 edition published at Valladolid, Spain.)   (5)

[273] Sheehan, Bernard. 1973. *Seeds of Extinction: Jeffersonian Philanthropy and the American Indian.* New York: W. W. Norton. (21, 50)

[274] ———. 1980. *Savagism and Civility: Indians and Englishmen in Colonial Virginia.* London: Cambridge University Press.   (21)

[275] Sirmans, M. Eugene. 1966. *Colonial South Carolina: A Political History, 1663–1763.* Chapel Hill: University of North Carolina Press.   (33)

[276] Smith, Hale G. 1956. *The European and the Indian: European-Indian Contacts in Georgia and Florida.* Florida Anthropological Society Publications 4. Gainesville: E. O. Painter for the University of Florida.   (16)

[277] Smith, Hale G., and Mark Gottlob. 1978. "Spanish-Indian Relationships: Synoptic History and Archaeological Evidence, 1500–1763." In *Tacachale,* ed. J. T. Milanich and S. Proctor, pp. 1–18. See [200].   (16)

[278]   Smith, Paul H. 1964. *Loyalists and Red-coats: A Study in British Revolutionary Policy*. Chapel Hill: University of North Carolina Press.   (42)

[279]   Solís de Merás, Gonzalo. 1923 [1567]. *Pedro Menéndez de Avilés, Adelantado, Governor and Captain-General of Florida: Memorial*. Translated by Jeannette Thurber Connor. Publications of the Florida State Historical Society 3. Deland: Florida State Historical Society. Also see [194].   (11)

[280]   Sosin, Jack M. 1966. "The British Indian Department and Dunmore's War." *Virginia Magazine of History and Biography* 74:34–50.   (38)

[281]   ———. 1967. *The Revolutionary Frontier*. New York: Holt, Rinehart and Winston.   (40)

[282]   Starkey, Marion. 1946. *The Cherokee Nation*. New York: Knopf. Reprinted, New York: Russell and Russell, 1972.   (57)

[283]   Starr, J. Barton. 1976. "Campbell Town: French Huguenots in British West Florida." *Florida Historical Quarterly* 54:532–47.   (38)

[284] Strickland, Rennard. 1970. "Christian Gottlieb Priber: Utopian Precursor of the Cherokee Government." *Chronicles of Oklahoma* 48:264–79.   (49)

[285] ———. 1975. *Fire and the Spirits: Cherokee Law from Clan to Court.* Norman: University of Oklahoma Press.   (48)

[286] Sturtevant, William C. 1962. "Spanish-Indian Relations in Southeastern North America." *Ethnohistory* 9:41–94.   (13)

[287] ———. 1971. "Creek into Seminole." In *North American Indians in Historical Perspective,* ed. Eleanor Leacock and Nancy O. Lurie, pp. 92–128. New York: Random House.   (56)

[288] ———. 1979. "The Cherokee Frontiers, the French Revolution, and William Augustus Bowles." In *Cherokee Indian Nation: A Troubled History,* ed. Duane H. King. Knoxville: University of Tennessee Press.   (45)

[289] Swanton, John Reed. 1911. *Indian Tribes of the Lower Mississippi Valley and Adjacent Coast of the Gulf of Mexico.* Bureau of American Ethnology Bulletin 43. Wash-

ington, D.C.: Government Printing
Office.   (8)

[290]   ———. 1922. *Early History of the Creek
Indians and Their Neighbors.* Bureau of
American Ethnology Bulletin 73. Wash-
ington, D.C.: Government Printing
Office.   (8)

[291]   ———. 1931. *Source Material for the Social and Ceremonial Life of the Choctaw
Indians.* Bureau of American Ethnology
Bulletin 103. Washington, D.C.: Gov-
ernment Printing Office.   (8)

[292]   ———. 1932. "The Ethnological Value
of the De Soto Narratives." *American Anthropologist,* n.s., 34:570–90.   (7)

[293]   ———. 1939. *Final Report of the United
States De Soto Expedition Commission.* 76
Congr., 1st Sess., House Doc. 71. Wash-
ington, D.C.: Government Printing
Office.   (7)

[294]   ———. 1946. *The Indians of the Southeastern United States.* Bureau of American Ethnology Bulletin 137. Washington, D.C.: Government Printing Office.   (xi,
1, 8)

[295]   ———. 1952. *The Indian Tribes of North America.* Bureau of American Ethnology Bulletin 145. Washington, D.C.: Government Printing Office. Reprinted, Washington, D.C.: Smithsonian Institution.   (2)

[296]   TePaske, John J. 1975. "The Fugitive Slave: Intercolonial Rivalry and Spanish Slave Policy, 1697–1764." In *Eighteenth Century Florida and Its Borderlands,* ed. Samuel Proctor, pp. 1–12. Gainesville: University of Florida Press.   (28)

[297]   ———. 1975. "Spanish Indian Policy and the Struggle for Empire in the Southeast, 1513–1776." In *Contest for Empire, 1500–1775: Proceedings of an Indian American Revolution Bicentennial Symposium,* ed. John B. Elliot, pp. 25–40. Indianapolis: Indiana Historical Society.   (13)

[298]   Theisen, Gerald, ed. 1972. *The Narrative of Álvar Núñez Cabeza de Vaca.* Translated by Fanny Bandelier with an introduction by John Francis Bannon, illustrated by Michael McCurdy, with Oviedo's version of the lost Joint Report presented to the Audiencia of

Santo Domingo, translated by Gerald
Theisen. Barre, Mass.: Imprint Society.   (5)

[299] Trimble, David B. 1956. "Christopher
Gist and the Indian Service in Virginia,
1757–59." *Virginia Magazine of History
and Biography* 64:143–65.   (38)

[300] Usner, Daniel H., Jr. 1951. "Frontier
Exchange in the Lower Mississippi Valley: Race Relations and Economic Life
in Colonial Louisiana, 1699–*1783.*"
Ph.D. diss., Duke University. Ann Arbor: University Microfilms.   (33)

[301] Valliere, Kenneth L. 1979. "The Creek
War of 1836: A Military History."
Chronicles of Oklahoma, winter, pp.
463–85.   (56)

[302] Van Der Beets, Richard, ed. 1973. *Held
Captive by Indians: Selected Captivity Narratives, 1642–1836.* Knoxville: University of Tennessee Press.   (35)

[303] Varner, John Grier, and Jeanette
Johnson Varner, trans. 1951. *The
Florida of the Inca: A History of the Adelantado Hernando de Soto, Governor and Captain General of the Kingdom of Florida, and*

of Other Heroic Spanish and Indian Cavaliers, Written by the Inca, Garcilaso de la Vega. Austin: University of Texas Press. Originally published as *La Florida del Ynca,* Lisbon: Pedro Crasbeeck, 1605. (7)

[304] Vaughan, Alden T. 1978. "'Expulsion of the Salvages': English Policy and the Virginia Massacre of 1622." *William and Mary Quarterly,* 3d ser., 35:57–84. (21)

[305] Voorges, Jacqueline K. 1976. "The Attakapas Post: The First Acadian Settlement." *Louisiana History* 17:91–96. (38)

[306] Wade, Mason. 1969. "The French and the Indians." In *Attitudes of Colonial Powers toward the American Indian,* ed. Howard Peckham and Charles Gibson, pp. 61–80. Salt Lake City: University of Utah Press. (32)

[307] Walker, Thomas. 1898. *Journal of an Exploration in the Spring of the Year 1750.* Boston: Little, Brown. (38)

[308] Washburn, Wilcomb E. 1957. *The Governor and the Rebel: A History of Bacon's Rebellion in Virginia.* Chapel Hill: University of North Carolina Press. (29)

[309]   ———. 1957. "Governor Berkeley and King Philip's War." *New England Quarterly* 30:363–77.   (29)

[310]   ———. 1959. "The Moral and Legal Justifications for Dispossessing the Indians." In *Seventeenth-Century America: Essays in Colonial History,* ed. James M. Smith, pp. 15–32. Chapel Hill: University of North Carolina Press.   (22)

[311]   ———. 1962. "The Effect of Bacon's Rebellion on Government in England and Virginia." *United States National Museum Bulletin* 225:135–52.   (29)

[312]   ———. 1965. "Indian Removal Policy: Administrative, Historical and Moral Criteria for Judging Its Success or Failure." *Ethnohistory* 12:274–78.   (52)

[313]   Watson, Thomas D. 1976. "Continuity in Commerce: Development of the Panton, Leslie, and Company Trade Monopoly in West Florida." *Florida Historical Quarterly* 54:548–64.   (45)

[314]   ———. 1976. "A Scheme Gone Awry: Bernardo de Galvez, Gilberto Antonio de Maxent, and the Southern Indian Trade." *Louisiana History* 17:5–17.   (45)

[315]   Wells, Robin F. 1973. "Frontier Systems as a Sociocultural Type." *Papers in Anthropology* 14:6–15.   (37)

[316]   Whitaker, Arthur P. 1927. *The Spanish American Frontier, 1783–1795.* Boston: Houghton Mifflin. Reprinted, Gloucester, Mass.: Peter Smith, 1962.   (47)

[317]   White, David H. 1975. "The Indian Policy of Juan Vicente Folch, Governor of Spanish Mobile, 1781–1792." *Alabama Review* 28:261–75.   (44)

[318]   ———. 1975. "The Spaniards and William Augustus Bowles in Florida, 1799–1803." *Florida Historical Quarterly* 54:145–55.   (45)

[319]   Willis, William S. 1963. "Divide and Rule: Red, White, and Black in the Southeast." *Journal of Negro History* 48:157–67.   (28)

[320]   Wood, Peter. 1974. *Black Majority: Negroes in Colonial South Carolina from 1670 through the Stono Rebellion.* New York: W. W. Norton.   (28)

[321]   Woods, Patricia D. 1978. "The French and the Natchez Indians in Louisiana,

1700–1731." *Louisiana History,* fall, pp. 413–35.   (33)

[322]   Woodward, Grace. 1963. *The Cherokees.* Norman: University of Oklahoma Press.   (57)

[323]   Wright, J. Leitch, Jr. 1964. "Spanish Reaction to Carolina." *North Carolina Historical Review* 41:464–76.   (30)

[324]   ———. 1967. *W. A. Bowles, Director General of the Creek Nation.* Athens: University of Georgia Press.   (45)

[325]   ———. 1971. *Anglo-Spanish Rivalry in North America.* Athens: University of Georgia Press.   (30, 38)

[326]   ———. 1975. *Florida in the American Revolution.* Gainesville: University of Florida Press.   (27)

[327]   ———. 1976. "Blacks in British East Florida." *Florida Historical Quarterly* 55:425–42.   (26)

[328]   ———. 1976. *Britain and the American Frontier, 1783–1815.* Athens: University of Georgia Press.   (38)

*[329] ———. 1981. *The Only Land They Knew: The Tragic Story of the Indians in the Old South.* New York: Free Press.   (xv)

[330] Yonge, Julian C., ed. 1938. "Hernando De Soto Number." *Florida Historical Quarterly*, vol. 16, no. 3. Includes John R. Swanton, "The Landing Place of De Soto"; James A. Robertson, trans., "Letter of De Soto to the Secular Cabildo of Santiago de Cuba"; "Concession Made by the King of Spain to De Soto"; Mark F. Boyd, "The Arrival of De Soto's Expedition in Florida"; and "Letter to the King of Spain from Officers in De Soto's Army."   (6)

[331] Young, Mary E. 1955. "The Creek Frauds: A Study in Conscience and Corruption." *Mississippi Valley Historical Review* 42:411–37.   (51)

[332] ———. 1961. *Redskins, Ruffleshirts, and Rednecks: Indian Allotments in Alabama and Mississippi, 1830–1860.* Norman: University of Oklahoma Press.   (52)

[333] ———. 1972. "Indian Removal and Land Allotment: The Civilized Tribes and Jacksonian Justice." *American Historical Review* 64:31–45.   (52)

[334]   ———. 1975. "Indian Removal and the Attack on Tribal Autonomy: The Cherokee Case." In *Indians of the Lower South: Past and Present,* ed. John K. Mahon. Pensacola: Gulf Coast History and Humanities Converence.   (51)

[335]   Zahendra, Peter. 1976. "Spanish West Florida, 1781–1821." Ph. D. Diss., University of Michigan Ann Arbor. University Microfilms.   (47)

[336]   Zubillaga, Félix. 1941. *La Florida: La misión Jesuítica (1566–1572) y la colonización española.* Roma: Institutum Historicum, S.J.   (14)

[337]   ———, ed. 1946. *Monumenta Antiquae Floridae (1566–1572).* Missiones Occidentales 3. Rome: Societatis Iesu.   (14)

The Newberry Library
Center for the History of the American Indian
Founding Director: D'Arcy McNickle
Director: Francis Jennings

Established in 1972 by the Newberry Library, in conjunction with the Committee on Institutional Cooperation of eleven midwestern universities, the Center makes the resources of one of America's foremost research libraries in the Humanities available to those interested in improving the quality and effectiveness of teaching American Indian history. The Newberry's collections include some 110,000 volumes on the history of the American Indian and offer specialized resources for studying historical aspects of Indian-White relations and Indian linguistics. The Center also assists Native Americans engaged in writing tribal histories and developing educational materials.

ADVISORY COMMITTEE

Chairman: Alfonso Ortiz
University of New Mexico